PLAYING BY
heart

Leon Gibbs
And The Miller Brothers Band

PLAYING BY
heart

Leon Gibbs
And The Miller Brothers Band

Carroll Wilson

MIDWESTERN STATE UNIVERSITY PRESS
WICHITA FALLS, TEXAS

Dedicated to my biggest fan, my very patient wife, Lynda, and to the memory of Malcolm Helm.

ACKNOWLEDGMENTS

Many very kind and helpful people made this book possible. First, Leon Gibbs, the man at the center of the story that is told here, made himself and all his diaries and notebooks available from the outset. Over about a year and a half, we talked a total of about 80 hours specifically about his life and his music, and we spent countless other hours playing, singing and writing music together. Getting to know him has been one of the highlights of my life, and I will always cherish his friendship. I am particularly grateful to Frances Tate, who patiently listened to and transcribed the tapes of my conversations with Leon. Hers was a thankless task, mainly because of the poor quality of the recordings, which were made in Leon's small studio at Sam Gibbs Music Co. while piano lessons were being taught on one side of us and bass lessons on the other. Likewise, special thanks go to Gary Lawson, photo chief of the Times Record News, for the photographs he has provided for the book; and to Julie Gaynor of the Times Record News design staff for her creative design for the book cover. Thanks, too, to Denise Nelson of the newspaper for her photo imaging. I have been fortunate indeed to have the poet laureate of Texas, James Hoggard, professor of English at Midwestern State University, as my editor. He has made me look very good on paper. To all those who provided clippings, photos and memories to help me complete this work, I do appreciate your many kindnesses.

CONTENTS

INTRODUCTION

This story is about the Gibbs brothers and the fabulous Miller Brothers Band. It's way overdue and sure is welcome.

The Miller Brothers inspired me personally when I watched them perform at the M-B Corral in Wichita Falls for a radio broadcast in 1957, when I was privileged to get to hear the great band leader and fiddler, Leon Gibbs. Just one year later, after joining Bob Will's band I discovered Leon's brother Sam Gibbs was managing the great Texas Playboys band. Later in the 60s, I got real lucky and had the pleasure of working with Leon Gibbs with the Texas Playboys band after I was hired as band leader. These associations were priceless to me and I'm so anxious to read their story.

What a musical career and what a legacy they left for us to enjoy. Read on! This is gonna be good!

— Leon Rausch, former Texas Playboys band leader, summer 2002

PREFACE

My best friend growing up in Amarillo, Texas, in the 50s and 60s was a kid with a natural ear and talent for music who played trombone in the marching bands at Austin Junior High and Amarillo High School and also guitar because it was the popular music instrument of the day.

Folk music was all the rage on the radio and in the music shops, and my buddy Malcolm Helm had the amazing ability to simply listen to a song – even broadcast over AM radio – and then sit down and play it, and play it well on guitar. And if the pitch didn't match his singing range, he could transpose the music on the spot in his head so he could sing it.

Malcolm was so good that as a junior in high school, he was teaching guitar lessons for cash at The Nizzi Music Shop.

I, too, loved music, particularly the folk music of Bob Dylan, Peter, Paul & Mary, Ian and Sylvia, and Joan Baez. I desperately wanted to learn to play guitar like Malcolm, even though he and I both knew I couldn't "hear" music well enough to ever play very well. So Malcolm taught me at a discounted rate.

Even though I took lessons from Malcolm for more than a year, we never delved into how to read music on the printed page or how to write music. I was actually satisfied learning chords and songs and was eminently pleased that literally hundreds of songs from that era could be played if you just knew a handful of chords to strum on the guitar. Knowing how to make the chords G, C, D7, F, E, Em and Am could get you passably through a folk-rock repertory of amazing proportions.

Malcolm taught me finger-picking patterns and interesting strums, and after our senior year, when we went in separate directions, I had all the skills I thought I needed to play for family and friends. After all, I never intended to be a real musician and never intended to perform in public.

So I didn't practice much, didn't play much and even sold my guitar, a Martin D18, to a friend before going into the Army in 1970.

When I got out of the service in 1972, I had a pocketful of mustering-out money so upon returning to Amarillo I bought a Gibson Heritage guitar with the intention of starting to play again. By that time I had a 2-year-old daughter, and I thought she'd get a kick out of singing along with her dad. She wouldn't care if he was any good on the instrument or not.

Over the course of the next several years, I revisited the songs I'd known in high school and tracked down some song books that helped refresh my memory. Musically, I was stuck in the 60s folk era, which was just fine with my growing family. By the end of the 70s I had three daughters.

Many nights we would sit around the coffee table in the living room of our little house in Canyon, Texas, where I was editor and associate publisher of the semi-weekly newspaper. My family sang while I played.

The girls loved those moments of closeness and musical harmony, and so did I. Then an enormous sadness replaced those warm interludes. My wife and I divorced and she retained custody of the girls. With no one to play for, I put my guitar in a closet and left it there, untouched, for almost 15 years. That loss was somehow reinforced when Malcolm Helm died in 1991. All the idea of playing the guitar did was make me want to cry.

As many others do when they turn 50, I started reflecting on my life. Lolling around in thoughts of grief and loss and dreadful limitations, I dwelled on the things

I regretted and shortchanged what I had to celebrate.

More and more I found myself regretting not having kept up with the guitar. Worse, I regretted not having learned to read music. I felt subliterate. How could I improve? How could I learn new material? How could I grow? I didn't care that I probably wouldn't ever get good enough to play publicly. Every time I looked at a song in a hymnal at church I felt frustrated. I couldn't make heads or tails out of the musical notation. But I still couldn't give up.

One Saturday in 1999, I took my old Gibson Heritage guitar to Sam Gibbs Music Co. in Wichita Falls to have the strings replaced and the parts checked out.

Then another Saturday, I took off in search of a guitar teacher in Wichita Falls who had time to show me how to read music and to reacquaint me with the guitar. I landed back at Sam Gibbs Music Co., where I was told that Leon Gibbs had an opening on Tuesday afternoons that I could fill. I signed up.

At that point, I knew next to nothing about Leon Gibbs, other than that he must be related to the Sam Gibbs who had his name on the music store. I figured Leon might be in his 20s or 30s.

Likewise, at that point I knew next to nothing about The Miller Brothers. I had read an occasional story about the group, and I knew they had some connection to a dance hall called the M-B Corral where Elvis had once played.

When I arrived for my first lesson Leon's apparent age surprised me (he even turned out to be older than he looked). Even more, his warmth, his knowledge and his gentle style of teaching amazed me.

Though it was hard for me to believe, as the weeks rolled by, I found myself catching on to how to read music. With Leon's help, I also learned I could even write some songs myself. He was building my confidence, and my playing improved.

I didn't, however, get lost in myself. More than anything else I found myself yearning to know more about a man who had obviously had a musical career of some note, a man with a big talent for stringed instruments, a man who was brilliant as a teacher. So I started asking him questions, and quickly found out that he had been the leader and lead fiddle player for a Western Swing group called The Miller Brothers. Not only that, he was also part owner of the M-B Corral. He'd been a contemporary of Bob Wills and had even played as a member of the Texas Playboys.

"Wow, what a great story!" I found myself thinking.

Yeah, I told myself, one that's so good it's probably already been told. But by whom?

I checked the public library and the Midwestern State University Library and also went through the files at the Wichita Falls *Times Record News*, where I'm editor. With the exception of some mentions in books, like the one on Bob Wills by Dr. Charles Townsend, a friend of mine from what's now West Texas A&M University, there were only scattered yellowed clippings that I could find about The Miller Brothers. I set out to change that.

Initially, pulling information out of Leon was difficult. That part of his life was behind him, and he was happy teaching and playing upon occasion. Still, he gave me enough of the Gibbs brothers' story to engage my curiosity.

Along about that same time, Leon was getting letters and phone calls from writers in other parts of the world wanting to tell his story, and I frankly encouraged him not to cooperate unless he absolutely knew that he'd get something out of the deal. After all, it was *his* story.

Right at the first of 2001, Leon and I were talking

about his past, and I offered to tell his story – with his help. He agreed, so we started weekly taped interview sessions, and I began collecting as much additional material as I could find.

Thankfully, prior to that Leon had begun writing down notes in a journal, chronicling his life and the life of the band and the M-B Corral. As we talked, he drew on those hand-written diaries to help refresh his memory as we talked. In addition, he had kept plenty of photos from The Miller Brothers days, and they were still in good shape.

Nat Gibbs, one of Leon's older twin brothers, came to Wichita Falls for an interview and also provided other background. Unfortunately, though, Leon's other older twin brother, Sam, who was a pioneering booking agent for bands and also a member of the original Miller Brothers, was unable to participate in the research I conducted for this book. By the time Leon and I got the project under way, Sam was afflicted with Alzheimer's disease.

A musician, critic and music historian, Don Chance of Dallas had conducted a taped interview with Leon and Sam in 1999, and I was able to draw on that session to a limited extent. Don also wrote a monograph at my request about the band and about Sam's booking agency, and I'm indebted to him for those materials. Newspaper clippings from the *Times Record News* files gave me more information.

Even though Sam was booking agent for Wills and his groups for 15 years, Charles Townsend only mentioned Sam in passing in his classic work on Bob Wills. That means there are inevitable holes in this book and probably some unanswered questions.

What I hope has been revealed, though, is something more than a few lines about a group of guys who got together to make music that had people up and dancing. The story of Leon Gibbs and his brothers is the story of how people who are willing to work long hours at tough jobs can overcome hard times, commit to something bigger than themselves and accomplish much more than they ever dreamed possible.

The Gibbs boys grew up in the Great Depression and came of age in the Army and Navy during World War II. When they got back to Wichita Falls, they built lives of extraordinary influence. They weren't whiners or loafers; they were do-ers.

In his book *The Greatest Generation,* Tom Brokaw writes of others who similarly made their way through most of the 20th century:

"It may be historically premature to judge the greatness of a whole generation, but indisputably, there are common traits that cannot be denied. It is a generation that, by and large, made no demands of homage from those who followed and prospered economically, politically, and culturally because of its sacrifices. It is a generation of towering achievement and modest demeanor, a legacy of their formative years when they were participants in and witness to sacrifices of the highest order." (*Greatest Generation* 11)

In my book, I pay homage to the Gibbs boys and all their contemporaries who have enriched my life and those of so many of my and my children's generations.

— Carroll Wilson, 2003

CHAPTER 1

Even into his 80s, Leon Gibbs could remember the way a song sounded when he and the Miller Brothers Band played it for an audience or for a recording session.

Strumming his aging Martin Sigma sunburst guitar as he sat in the small teaching studio he used at Sam Gibbs Music Co. in Wichita Falls, he'd shuffle through the thousands of tunes that must linger inside his very active mind, hum a little, and then find the notes and chords he was looking for. Off he'd go, encouraging the student to watch his hands and follow.

The student might want more than this mere taste of that swinging Miller Brothers style, but until the spring of 2002 that just wasn't going to happen.

Leon had none of the more than 50 recordings he and his band produced on the Four Star label.

Nor did he have any sheet music or notes.

He just had memories.

In the spring of 2002, though, Leon found that he and the band had been rediscovered, and it was no longer just the stuff of his memory, those tunes played decades before by a group that hadn't stood together on stage in more than 35 years.

Early in the spring, one of Leon's guitar students came into the music store to show Leon a compact disc she had purchased from a site she had found after doing a search using his band's name on the Internet.

The sales staff photocopied the label information while Leon looked over the album notes included as part of the package.

Later, when he mentioned that his band's music was back in circulation, Leon wondered out loud where the company had gotten hold of the performances recorded on the CD and where they got permission to use the music for a profit.

The CD offered up 27 songs that at one time had been recorded by the Miller Brothers, many of which were written by Leon, including the once-popular "Loco Choo Choo," "Alligator Rag," "Tuning the Fiddle," "Woodchuck Boogie," "Hey Pretty Baby" and "Ramblin' Around."

On the cover of the package was a black-and-white photo of the Miller Brothers Band, and above that a poster from a band performance in Marietta, Georgia.

But the CD package also included a small eight-page CD-sized set of album notes detailing the history of the band and its recording career and showing five more photos of the band as a group posing in different venues. The notes appeared without giving credit to the responsible author. And no credits were given for the photos.

Leon was more perplexed than concerned.

Who held the copyright to the material? he was asked.

He seemed unsure.

Did he own them or have proof of ownership that he might have put away somewhere?

No.

Did Four Star?

Out of business.

Did he ever receive any royalties?

Not any more, not in a long time.

Had he ever signed anything assigning the copyright to the songs he wrote?

He didn't think so.

The CD in question could be ordered directly from a company calling itself Collector Records. It was billed at the company web site as a part of the "Boppin' Hillbilly Series." Payment could only be made in some form of currency other than a credit card.

More copies of the CD were ordered and arrived in mid-spring.

At first Leon wouldn't listen to them. He just seemed uninterested.

Then one day several members of the sales staff had the CD turned on and up loud enough for him to hear the music as he passed through the store to his studio, and he stopped and listened for awhile.

As the tunes played one after the other, he smiled, but he didn't stay to hear all of them.

"Gosh," he said as he walked away, "I sure remembered us sounding better than that."

He was, though, as unconcerned about the quality of the product as he was about the loss of a few dollars to someone overseas who had packaged his work.

This guy's making money off your legacy, he was told more than once. Don't you want to try to stop them or at least make them pay you a royalty?

Not really, Leon would say.

Not even a letter just to warn them away?

Naw.

Pretty soon, the subject was dropped until it came up again several weeks later, when Leon said that he remembered a fellow recording the band's entire performance one evening in Memphis, Tennessee, or, he said, maybe it was in Arkansas.

"Maybe that's where that came from," he surmised.

But that's as far as it went. And that's as far as he cared to see it go.

For 70 years he had been a maker of music, not money.

Neither fame nor fortune had been part of the plan.

CHAPTER 2

T he year Leon Gibbs was born, the United States was beginning to roar.

The "war to end all wars" had, in fact, ended just a few years before, but the Congress waited until 1921 to officially declare the cessation of hostilities. The nation was beginning to turn inward, and families were growing. In 1921, the average household size in the United States was 4.6 people, and 23 percent of the country's population was under the age of 10, setting the stage for a youth explosion during the decade that came to be called "The Roaring 20s" *(American Chronicle)*.

The movies in 1921 were still in black-and-white, and they were still silent, except for the piano or organ played in the movie house itself. Mary Pickford, Rudolph Valentino, Douglas Fairbanks, Wallace Reid and Gloria Swanson held sway over the masses who would go downtown on a Saturday afternoon to see a matinee. Those inclined to read could pick and choose from a large number of authors who we would say in retrospect were creators of the classics of 20th century literature. Best-sellers included *Main Street* by Sinclair Lewis, *The Age of Innocence* by Edith Wharton. Other notable works were *Notes and Reviews* by Henry James, *The Outline of History* by H.G. Wells and poetry by T.S. Eliot. Meanwhile, Eliot and Ezra Pound, Ernest Hemingway and F. Scott Fitzgerald, among others, left this country for Europe, setting up a haven for expatriates and writers. Mounds bars made their first appearance in 1921, as did Eskimo Pies and Betty Crocker, Wrigley's chewing gum, Band-Aids, Drano and the Lincoln automobile (*American Chronicle*).

The Wichita Falls of 1921 was likewise on a tear.

The city, which even then was the shopping and cultural hub of more than 17 counties in North Central Texas, had just experienced a growth spurt of shocking proportions. In 1910, the city population stood at 8,200. By 1920, the population had skyrocketed to 40,079, an increase of 389 percent, "placing it among the very first communities in the United States in percentage of population gain" (*Times* brochure). The population growth was almost all in numbers of Anglos, with the Census Bureau reporting only 2,372 "Negroes" in the community, or less than 3.8 percent. By contrast, the U.S. Census showed the city's Anglo population 80 years later, in 2000, was about 75 percent, the African American population was about 12 percent, and the Hispanic population about 14 percent.

What fueled that phenomenal growth in Wichita Falls? The oil boom of the teens. Oil was discovered in the immediate area in 1911, and that year alone 889,600 barrels of oil were produced in Wichita County. The Burkburnett oil field was discovered in 1918, adding tremendously to both the total production and also to the population. By 1921, the total annual production had grown to 24.2 million barrels (*Times* brochure).

Wichitans approached the new decade with optimism, and things were going so well in Wichita Falls in the early 20s that the *Wichita Falls Times* was prompted to declare in a brochure that "Wichita Falls is a good place to live. It is a city of beautiful and artistic homes, fine churches and progressive schools."

In 1921, though, oil prices went into a slump, and the Central Stock Exchange at 714 Ohio closed its doors, the last of five stock trading establishments in Wichita Falls to dissolve. In addition, three 10-coach trains that had been running every day between Wichita Falls and

Burkburnett were canceled ("Fifty Years").

In the midst of this rampant change, Leon Gibbs was born right outside of the east city limits on a 6.5-acre farm that was just a stone's throw from today's U.S. 287 and East Scott Avenue. Today, the dirt road meanders off Scott to cut east and south, going past a salvage yard, over a rail line and beside a low area that sometimes collects runoff water. The visitor passes by what Leon describes as the McKinney farm, owned by a family that had a stock tank the kids were allowed to swim in. When the Gibbs family fell onto hard times in the mid-20s, members of the McKinney family "knew our situation and would give us cookies and stuff any time we passed by." On the west side of the road in front of what was once the Gibbs farm is a housing development with rundown fences, unpainted exteriors and unkempt yards. To the east, the land is flat, probably good for cultivation at one time. But Leon remembered life there as hard and spare. The house where Walter Gibbs and Occie Delma Farley Gibbs set about to bring up Clyde, born in 1907, and C.L, born in 1901, and Nat and Sam, twin boys born 10 minutes apart in May of 1918, Leon, born in 1921, and Juanita, born in 1923, is no longer standing.

"We had a cistern by the back door," he recalled, "and it was a dang good one with concrete on the sides. Well, it went dry, and we did not have any water. We hauled in all the water to drink and bathe. Mama boiled the water so we could drink it. We just had a terrible time getting water."

Leon believes that his dad, Walter Gibbs, who came with Leon's mother to Wichita County in the teens from Carthage, Tennessee, was a pretty good farmer (he owned his own threshing machine), but his dad also worked in the oil field and made a relatively comfortable living for the growing family. Leon and brother Nat remembered their dad driving home in the evenings in a new convertible, with the top down, allowing them to sit on the fender to hitch a ride part of the way home. They also recalled their dad allowing the two oldest brothers to use the car for dates. "We would get out there in that car early the next morning and look through the car to find pennies and nickels," Leon said.

While the image that experiences with the car draw to mind doesn't make it seem so, Leon and brother Nat agreed that their parents were tough task-masters.

Did his dad have a sense of humor?

"Not that I know of," Leon said. "Everything was strict."

Leon remembered a time when his family paid a visit to a woman and her children to pay their respects upon the death of the man in the family.

"And this little boy had one of those little pistols," Leon said. "I imagine he paid as much as 19 cents for it. I don't know, but I had to have that pistol so I absolutely stole that pistol."

How old was he?

"I was, say, five, because I can still remember this, but, boy, we got home and Mama found out I had this pistol. We took it back, and, man, they prayed over me, they touched hands on me, rebuked the Devil … I mean, you talk about laying hands on a person, Mama really laid hands on me. I never stole anything else again in my life, honestly. And I guess it was on account of that 19-cent pistol, but that actually happened."

That strict way of doing things was rooted in religion.

"Yes," Leon said, "we were big church members. We were all Pentecostal, brought up in the Pentecostal church, and, yes, they sang."

Even in public, the family practiced their faith.

"I can remember," Leon said, "my daddy going (to a restaurant that would be right across from what is today's Farmers Market at Eighth and Ohio in Wichita Falls) with all us kids on Sunday after church, and he would say thanks, and you could hear a pin drop in this restaurant, and then when he got through saying the prayer we could eat."

Leon had many memories of what it was like to go to one church at Fifth and Broad in Wichita Falls and then another church closer to the farm. After enduring one long service downtown, he remembers routinely being loaded into the back of a wagon for the trek to another church. His parents would pull all the children into the building, and make pallets for them because the services were lengthy.

"The first thing they would do is get to that altar and start praying, and many, many times we would sleep through it and Father would wake us," Leon said.

The church was on East Scott, according to Leon, who added without elaboration that the congregation was largely black. Interestingly, it appears that race was simply never an issue for Leon. When the family moved to town, he threw papers on the East Side, which in those days as now was largely populated with African Americans. And some of Leon's favorite bands and favorite musicians in his own group were Hispanic.

Those early years of church-going and praying and following rules strictly had a lasting impact on the Gibbs boys. More than Leon, Nat said he believed the impact was huge.

"My mother," Nat said, "I used to hear her praying every night. In cold weather when you live out in the country, she'd pray and we'd be so cold and the house would be so cold. We used a wood stove, and she had to make sock quilts, they weighed about 100 pounds, and we'd be sleeping and cold and she'd put an iron, two irons (heated and taken off the stove) so we could keep our feet on (them). And she prayed to the Lord for her boys. And that gave me so much comfort, really, all through my life, I don't think I've ever been smarter than anyone else, but I think to come from where we came from, to accomplish some of the things we accomplished, I think we had to have help. And I've always felt like that anything that I went into, that the Lord was going to take care of us. And He has, all of us, all of my life. He really took care of us."

It's probable, however, that no one in the family had that view in 1925 when the family's life took a radical turn. After being bitten by a black widow spider, Walter Gibbs died that year of pneumonia.

While Walter Gibbs had many assets, he also owed a great deal of money and had no savings, Leon said.

"In two months' time we started losing everything," he said. "The thrashing machine – gone; the car – gone. And Mama had a Singer sewing machine, and the man came to collect the last two payments. We kept the Singer, because she paid him with chickens."

The death of her spouse, the loss of the car, and everything else she owned stunned Mrs. Gibbs.

"You know, she never did anything when my daddy died," Leon said. "She stopped. She quit going to church. She quit going to PTA meetings that she always went to. She seemed to have just given up."

For a good five years, she never even cared if the children went to church, a radical departure from the past.

The loss of their dad and the situation with their mother meant that the boys had to go to work as soon as they could.

"We never felt like we had to work," Nat said, "I mean, had to. We knew we had to have the money, but in my whole life I have never hated having to go to work in the morning."

"We never did realize we were poor, you know that," added Leon.

"We didn't really take relief and all that, the free stuff," Nat continued. "One time a lady called the (welfare) office and said, 'You are trying to help people, why don't you help somebody who really needs it? There's a widow woman out here with four kids, three sons and a daughter, and I know they need help.' So the lady came out and she talked to my mother. She gave her chits or something, and you could take it to the store and get groceries. And so Mother took it and said, 'Look at what this lady gave us (whatever it was), and you boys need to go and pick it up (the groceries).' And we talked about it, and we decided we didn't need to do this – and she said, 'Well, the lady was nice enough to give us this, let's accept it.' Well, we cried. And so she said, 'If you'll pick these groceries up, I'll never ask you to do that again.' And I don't remember ever being asked to do that again."

Why would the boys resist help at a time when they needed it so desperately?

"We were just embarrassed to take anything," Leon said. "You had to go — walk — down to the auditorium to get the food, and we just hated having people look at us, and we worried that people would know where the food came from."

Then, reflecting on their attitude back then, he said, "We just knew we were going to have to work that much harder to keep from taking it."

CHAPTER 3

I t's safe to say that Leon Gibbs, with the exception of his early childhood, has never seen a period when he didn't need to or want to work.

While others might have retired at age 65, Leon never considered it, and was still working in his early 80s after the 20th century turned into the 21st, teaching young disciples how to play guitar or fiddle. He was an instructor at Sam Gibbs Music Co.

His has been a work ethic based first of all on necessity but also upon the sheer love of being active and productive. He learned those values the hard way as a child who came of age during the 1930s.

The advent of the Great Depression at the end of the 20s, however, couldn't have had much real impact on the struggling Gibbs family. They were already in a depression of their own.

Through the first half of that decade, they were living comfortably on a small farm east of Wichita Falls, thanks to the farming knowledge of Walter Gibbs.

But Walter's death in 1925 changed the family forever, and Mrs. Gibbs went into what was apparently a deep depression that prevented her from working at all. Nevertheless she hung onto the property until about 1928 when she sold it to a man for $650. The man wanted to pay the debt out over time. Mrs. Gibbs let him, but Leon said he remembered the man never paid off the full amount.

With the farm sold, the family, now including a girl, Juanita, moved to a house on Mississippi Street. A little later they moved again in the same area to a house at 408

Mississippi.

To make ends meet, even when living in the country east of town, Sam and Nat, the twins who were three years older than Leon, contracted with George Cochran of the *Wichita Falls Times* to sell newspapers as street hawkers. C.L., a brother who was older than the twins, went to work during the 30s with the Works Progress Administration and regularly sent money home.

Life was not particularly comfortable for the family of three brothers and a sister and their mother, but they managed to get by. And by the end of the decade, they were certainly not alone in seeing their wealth evaporate. Their introduction to austerity may have come a year earlier than it did for most. The stock market crash of 1929 shocked the entire nation, and Wichita Falls' economy felt the reverberations almost immediately.

A *Times* summary of headlines appearing in the papers in 1930 says many of them "reflected hardship and poverty, and community efforts to combat them," continuing:

> Buildings remaining at Call Field (the air force's base west of town) from the Texas-Oklahoma Fair were offered worthy poor families for living quarters. On March 11, there were an estimated 2,000 unemployed. Closing of the junior college was threatened. Family relief funds of $20,000 in the Community Chest represented more than a third of the total. The Red Cross maintained a drought relief office for six weeks to distribute seed rye, wheat and barley to nearly 6,000 farm families in 29 counties. (*Fifty Years*)

The following year was just as bad, with voters rejecting various civic improvements that would have increased taxes, and with teachers being paid only part of their salaries.

The *Times* retrospective further explained the dire situation: "The unemployed staged several meetings. A group identified as the 'Unemployed Council of Wichita Falls' paraded Aug. 1, and the *Daily Worker*, Communist Party newspaper, was sold by parade participants." Roving gangs of hungry people attacked one relief worker, and 20 people later raided the kitchen of the county jail (*Fifty Years*).

In that context, the Gibbs brothers were actually lucky. They had a house to call home, and they had jobs, even if it was just selling the daily newspaper.

"That is when you could buy a paper for three cents, sell it for a nickel and you had done made yourself two cents profit every time you sold one," Leon recalled. At the time, he hawked papers mainly by tagging along with Nat and Sam. "I mean, lordy mercy, on a good day you might sell five or six papers."

The three boys sold papers every day of the week, twice a day. In the mornings they would rise at 4 a.m. and trek to the newspaper offices at 719 Seventh and get papers to sell, stopping in time to get to school on the weekdays and about 9 a.m. on Sundays. In the afternoons after school, they were back downtown getting papers to sell until dark.

On Sundays, the boys would stay out until they had sold all their papers, Leon said, and every cent they made went to their mother after they had settled accounts with Cochran.

Not long after moving to the second address on Mississippi, the boys bought regular routes from George Cochran, routes that they could throw on a steady basis, seven days a week, twice a day except for Saturdays and Sundays. They now had regular routes with regular customers they would have to collect from.

Leon's route was altogether on the East Side of

Wichita Falls and included homes on Flood Street, Rosewood, along the tracks and around Spudder Park – an area he himself characterized as "all of colored town, and then the old dog pound and what used to be the incinerator." All in all, he believes he served 200 customers morning and evening every day.

In the 1930s, Wichita Falls' East Side was, in fact, the home of its small African American population.

Flood Street was "main street" for this group of citizens, and they had their own schools and their own businesses. The first "Negro" school, Booker T. Washington School, was opened in 1921 (*Fifty Years*).

In various published anecdotes, members of the African American community have painted a picture of social life on the East Side of Wichita Falls as one carried on almost entirely separately from life on the other side of the railroad tracks. Movie theaters and night clubs served their entertainment needs.

It would be unheard of today for a child of any race to deliver papers door to door anywhere in Wichita Falls, even in the afternoon, so it seems unusual that Leon would have thrown a route on the predominately minority East Side. According to him, he never had any trouble and, in fact, never thought twice about it, even when collecting. And collecting was part of the job.

"The paper was 20 cents a week if you paid by the week," Leon said, "or 75 cents a month. That's the way a lot of them paid. But when I sold to a new customer, if they wanted it by the week, I always suggested it, and I got 20 cents a week, which made me an extra nickel."

Just how much that extra nickel meant to him is illustrated in a couple of stories Leon told about his days on the paper route.

One arose from his days on the route he ran for George Cochran: "There used to be a barbecue stand over there, right where the colored part of town started, and one day my boss, George Cochran, said, 'I don't ever notice that you collect from these people. Don't they take the paper?' And I said, 'Yes sir, I trade the paper for a sandwich every week.' I thought I'd get in trouble, but he never said another word, and I did that the rest of the time – traded the paper for a week for a sandwich."

The other story Leon traced to that period when he was hawking papers: "We went into this restaurant and this guy – right down by the depot – and we ordered hot cakes, which would have cost us – we drank water – I forget what it would have cost – it would have been less than a dollar, and this guy remembered our daddy, that we always came in on Sunday and ate dinner after church. And my dad would always give thanks at the table when they would bring the food, and you could hear a pin drop – I remember this. I thought some day some smart aleck is going to make fun of him, but they didn't. It never happened. And this guy remembered our daddy giving thanks, and he never charged us for a meal."

While throwing routes and collecting, the boys were also attending school, Leon the old Barwise School, built in 1921, which later became a disciplinary unit for the school district known as Holland School on Jalonic Street off East Scott Street near the Jacksboro Highway intersection.

Did you ever feel like when you looked around the other kids were working as hard as you were? Leon was asked.

"Well," he responded, "they didn't have to, I don't guess. See, we were making a living."

Did you resent that?

"No," he said. "It's just the way it was. I don't ever remember blowing any money. I know Mama got us everything we needed or had to have. We ran a charge account on Seymour Street at Davenport's Grocery, that's when we all had the routes. And we charged everything and we paid them at least twice a month ... Life was pretty rough, really.

"I know one thing in school, when I got in high school – in the ninth grade, the teacher knew how we did, with this paper route. And somebody we knew had an old van and they would pick us up and take us to school. Anyway, this teacher was told how – what hours we worked – and during study period, which was in a big old room, just full of seats, two or three times bigger than a regular room, and this teacher would let me sleep, and I would put my head on this desk and go to sleep, and that teacher never woke me up. Someone had told her this, so I never did question it. Because after you made your paper route, and you'd get home, man, all you had time to do was wash your face and teeth because here's some kid out there honking, ready to go to school."

Later, Leon acquired other routes from the *Times* and *Record News*, including one long one that totaled about 200 customers between Seymour Highway and Seventh Street around the old Coyote Canyon football stadium.

Did he ever think, Good Lord, am I going to be throwing papers when I'm an old man?

"No," Leon said.

But he was still throwing papers and collecting for them when he was drafted into the U.S. Army in the early 1940s.

And he always sang the praises of the newspaper and George Cochran and others he worked for whose names he could not recall.

"Now you talk about somebody treated like royalty," Leon said of the newspaper circulation staff. "They treated us that way. Honest they did. We were something special, not just the Gibbs boys. Everybody was. And everybody stayed for years and years. I mean, they didn't come in, work a few months and go. Everyone was there to stay. It was real nice."

Throwing papers as a kid not even yet in his teenage years set the pace for Leon Gibbs and for his brothers, who continued through long decades to do more than just show up for work.

CHAPTER 4

A lthough the Gibbs brothers worked hard as youngsters growing up under depressed circumstances, they found at least one diversion. Leon could recall listening to a hand-crafted crystal radio set put together by one of his brothers, and remembers that most of the time it was tuned to KWFT, a local AM station that carried country and western music.

Even earlier, though, Nat remembered his mom listening to country musicians on a small radio that she had. He also recalled one particular musician whose tunes his mother loved and hearing her remark that he made $1,500 every performance. From that point on, he said, she determined that one or all of her children still at home would become musicians — even though not one of the brothers or their sister Juanita could find any evidence of any musical talent among any of their relatives or ancestors.

At the start of the Depression, about the time Leon was entering third grade, radios were still scarce in Texas. Census Bureau surveys at the time indicated that Oklahoma households were more likely to have radios than Texas households. But since Leon and family did have access to radio, they apparently kept it tuned to country music, which was just coming into its own across the nation.

Only a few years before, Jimmie Rodgers and The Carter Family had become the first nationally known 'hillbilly' recording stars (*A Century of Country* 35). By 1930, it's been estimated that 27 percent of Victor's record sales and 40 percent of a label called Gennett were coming from hillbilly and southern-gospel recordings (*A Century of Country* 35).

Collier's magazine ran a feature story on the phenomenon in 1929, and *Better Homes & Gardens* picked up on the trend for a piece in 1930 (*A Century of Country* 35).

The reason, according to these sources, was radio. As *A Century of Country* notes: "By this time the Depression had hit, and record sales were in a free fall, dropping from $46.2 million in 1930 to $17.6 million in 1931. They would continue to drop precipitously throughout the next two years. Radio, on the other hand, was booming. And with it boomed country music" (36). Millions of radio sets were manufactured and sold each year, and as radio stations learned what the public wanted, more country artists got on the air.

Regardless of what her interest might have been in getting one of her children involved in music and on the radio, to make $1,500 a night during the Depression years, Leon's mother did not influence the older Gibbs boys in that direction. According to Leon and Nat, it was actually just a fluke that Leon got into music at all.

Leon was pretty good at music in the early grades. While he made Ds and Cs in other classes, he made As in music, and he always liked to sing. One day in third grade, his teacher handed him a leaflet after class and it advertised violin lessons for 50 cents per one-hour lesson for a class of 12 students.

When he got the slip, he took it home and gave it to his mother, apparently oblivious of his family's money-strapped condition. When she said he couldn't take the lessons, he "cried and cried and cried."

"He wanted to play violin, and we were so poor my mother sold a sewing machine to pay for it," his sister remembered. "And when he started — anyway, it was very hard to do; we were poor. He wanted that violin and he got it."

No one could recall how much the violin cost Mrs. Gibbs, but the Sears & Roebuck catalog for the year 1932 lists the cost of a student outfit, which included a violin and several written lessons and some sheet music, at $7.95 without the case (Sears 497). To put that into perspective, $1 in 1932 was equal in value to $13.09 in the year 2002, according to a cost-of-living calculator (NewsEngin.com). Further perspective comes from the Sears catalog, which was selling boys' denim pants at $1.09, boy's shoes at $1.89, a voiles dress at $2.94 and an "official" baseball with horsehide covers at $1 each.

In those early days of the Great Depression, money was just plain hard to come by for most families in Wichita Falls, so the Gibbses weren't the exception.

In 1932, the Parent-Teachers Association inaugurated the free lunch program for needy students in the public schools, and one area dairy responded by donating 20,000 bottles of milk. A fund-raising campaign by the P-TA raised enough to pay the nickel per lunch needed to make the program work. Still, the schools, along with other public bodies, were forced to cut expenses, some by as much as 25 percent, and one local government defaulted on its bonds (*Times Record News* 50th anniversary edition).

It must have been a frustrated Mrs. Gibbs who found that after she'd paid for Leon to become a musician, he decided he'd rather not practice. "I don't know why I wanted to play because before very long I was crying to quit," Leon wrote in his own notes. "Mama wouldn't let me." Instead, she was apparently determined to see him not just learn to play but to learn to play well.

In fact, Nat's recollection was that she taught herself how to read music so she could stay just far enough ahead of Leon to drill him when he came home. She would sit him on a bucket and sit down with him while he played and go over the notes he was to learn.

"We had an old wind-up record player and all kinds of songs," Leon said. "I learned a lot from those records, and I learned a lot from the radio — fast. If the old record player got slower, I learned you were dragging — wind it up. And at first it would be rushing. I learned real quick about tempo and timing."

Leon, though, took lessons in the formal class of 12 students for only eight or nine months, because the family simply couldn't afford the 50 cents every week.

Leon's playing, however, had apparently caught the attention of a man named Stanley Myles Raub, who was a classical violinist and teacher who took Leon under his wing, telling the boy he would teach him to play if Leon would play in his recitals.

Before long, Leon was learning classical pieces by reading and hearing the music, but he was also caught up in teaching himself to play country music simply by listening to the radio and records.

More than that, though, he was helping to teach Sam how to play guitar and Nat how to play standup bass.

"I wanted somebody to play with, and I got them interested in it," Leon said.

A family friend and musically talented young man, J.E. Gose, actually sat the twins down and taught them to play their instruments by ear. It was Leon who later sat them down to teach them how to read music. Together, they formed a trio that had an insatiable appetite for music. One of the first places they ventured to play together was a Pentecostal church on Holliday Street led by Brother S.D. Doyle, where the family had a charter membership.

Mamie Caywood led the singing, with Leon on fiddle, Sam on guitar, Nat on bass, Harrold Lee on banjo,

Frank Looney on guitar and Ruth Doyle on piano.

"She played like Jerry Lee Lewis does now, and she played that way then," Leon said. "The choir, which was anyone who wanted to sing, and this swinging band made the rafters rock. We always went to play at church on Sunday night and most of the Wednesday night services."

While the brothers devoted some time to religious music, they recognized early on that the money was in country, and that was the direction they intended to go.

"We found out earlier that money was in Western Swing," Leon said. "And we found that out by watching Bob Wills."

Bob Wills was a major influence on the musical style Leon and his brothers adopted and nurtured, particularly Leon, as he copied the style that made Wills's music so different and so popular.

Wills and others called it "Western Swing," but few could define it. You almost had to hear it to understand — not the "western" part, but the "swing" part.

Some trace Western Swing to the actual strain of music called Swing:

When (Louis) Armstrong published a book about jazz in 1936, he called it 'Swing that Music' and argued that 'swing' was the basic principle of New Orleans jazz. The main difference in the new swing music, he maintained, was that it used scored orchestrations, more sophisticated harmonies and more highly trained musicians. The problem, then, may have been simply to keep the basic characteristics of jazz while incorporating these new features of bigness, complexity, and written orchestrations. Today, long after the great vogue of swing bands, musicians, when they hear modern jazz in any style, continue to ask, 'Does it swing?' And the query is evidently synonymous with, 'Is it really jazz?'. (*America's Music: The Growth of Jazz* 479)

To understand the two idioms — "western" and "swing" — you have to understand how Wills, who grew up in the Turkey, Texas, Quitaque, Texas, region, took an amalgam of musical sources — his own musically-inclined family, the blacks he was around in the cotton patch, what he heard on the radio — and turned them into something unique. As Wills's primary and most respected biographer explained it:

> The blues idiom in his fiddle style helped give Wills's music the 'heat of jazz' that was a necessity in popular dance music in his generation. And in spite of his long, smooth bow strokes, which were conducive to a mournful blues quality, his use of syncopated rhythms gave his music the 'bumpiness' or 'swing' of jazz that characterized the popular jazz music of his age. The jazz in Wills's fiddle was not characterized by the hot breaks or hot choruses that Joe Venuti and Jesse Ashlock so brilliantly improvised. Wills nearly always played melody, giving it his own blues and jazz interpretation. This accounts, in part, for his popularity as a fiddler, since the average listener appreciated the melody more than the improvisation of the jazz choruses Wills always demanded from his musicians. ... Fortunately for Wills, about the time most jazz bands and dance orchestras were abandoning the violin, he began to revive it in dance music. He did much more, however. He made it a frontline instrument, often featuring from two to six violins in his fiddle ensemble... Wills made the fiddle and western music both popular and respectable. (*San Antonio Rose* 40-41)

Don Chance, a professional musician, music historian and music critic, had a slightly different view of the development and distinctive elements of Western Swing:

While many longtime fans tend to think the distinctive brand of Western Swing that was born and nurtured to popularity in the dance halls and roadhouses of circa-late 1930s West Texas and Oklahoma was merely a more primitive, fiddle-based version of the horn-driven 'Big Band' swing sound as popularized by Benny Goodman, the Dorsey Brothers, and so on, they are mostly mistaken. Outside the fact that both styles were intended primarily as dance music, the two sounds really don't share a common core ancestry when studied closely. (Don Chance 1)

As far as Chance is concerned, an abiding and important difference lay in the way the musicians in each idiom approached music on the printed page.

Horn players during the Big Band era usually needed at least some formal musical education to work together properly in the ensemble and light orchestral situations popular for the first half of the 20th century. Trumpets, trombones, saxophones, clarinets — all single-note wind instruments — are designed and built to operate best within just a few closely defined concert pitch keys, and the players must follow strictly notated charts to keep the ensemble sound together. (Chance 1)

While soloists were encouraged to improvise, they would immediately return to the written score as soon as the solo ended. In Western Swing bands, though, nothing quite so tight and regimented was thought necessary and many fiddlers, guitar players and pianists couldn't even read music, just as Nat and Sam of The Miller Brothers tended to play mostly by ear.

This freedom from the written page often means that the non-horn players tend to develop keener senses of timing, harmony and improvisation than most of their note-bound colleagues. But with this unique freedom comes unique responsibilities. Instead of depending on pre-written sheet music and formal conductors to keep them together, the musically uneducated country 'pickers' of the Big Band era developed the remarkable level of self-discipline necessary to compete on the same level with more formally trained players. But, just like the horn players, fiddlers such as Leon Gibbs might take off on a sizzling and instantly improvised solo when their turn came, but they instinctively returned to their group duties at the end of the solo. (Chance 2)

Regardless of the roots of the sound, it was the sound of Western Swing that Leon listened to so he could incorporate it into his own growing repertoire of songs, and that's probably the sound he pulled out of his fiddle when the boys got their first paying job as a trio.

That first gig was at a frozen custard stand on Eighth Street about a block from the General Hospital. The pay was $1 each for one and one-half hours of playing, with two 15-minute intermissions. In addition to the pay, they also each got an ice cream cone in the bargain. That job lasted one summer.

"We played a little bit of everything because I was studying classical music," Leon said. "Of course, we could play country music, whatever was popular that day. I do not know why, but if I ever heard it, I got to where I could play it. That is just like now — if I have heard it I can play it."

Before that first "job," though, the boys had plenty of practice at their church and also at the Boys Club on Ohio Street near a fire station that was located there at that time.

Marvin "Lefty" Robertson, head of the club, recruited them to play on Sunday mornings, and the brothers started regularly playing and singing for Sunday school at the club.

Before long, the Gibbs brothers had been recruited to play for hoe-downs at various locations and for square dances at the Country Club.

Leon recalls that it was a Dr. Josh Kimbrough who came to the Boys Club and liked what he heard out of the Gibbs boys.

They had joined a glee club that sang on Sundays put together by George Taylor, who was in charge of the music. The club's managers apparently realized that many youngsters during the Depression years were out working at odd hours and needed a place to congregate even on Sundays. "We learned a lot from George Taylor," Leon recalls. "He played guitar and sang."

But Dr. Kimbrough took a special interest in the boys.

"One time I went into the hospital," Leon said. "I had pneumonia, and he was my doctor. He told the nurses to take care of me, that I was a special young man. They did, too. When they released me, Mama went to the hospital office to tell them that we would have to pay by the month. We didnít have the money. The office manager told Mama that it was already taken care of, thanks to Dr. Josh Kimbrough."

Dr. Kimbrough encouraged the boys not to sell themselves short.

"He just knew we needed it, and he said, 'You boys need to start charging.'"

The boys' second playing job was at the Wichita Restaurant on Eighth Street. Again, they played one and one-half hours, from 7 p.m. to 8:30 p.m. and received $1 apiece plus a free meal. A meal in those days cost 35 cents.

Not long after the boys started making money at their music, Leon stopped taking lessons in the classics from Stanley Myles Raub, the man who had offered Leon lessons if Leon would play in his recitals. (Leon credited Raub with keeping him focused on regular practices and with an appreciation for music other than country and western.)

While they were finally getting paid for their talents, the boys were also taking non-paying jobs at the Elks Club and the Lions Club and the Rotary Club, probably because with Leon as the violinist they were something of an oddity with a prodigy in tow.

"We played a little bit of everything because I was studying classical music," Leon said.

Besides listening to radio, the boys also picked up music from others in the community. J.E. Gose was a good family friend, a little older than Nat and Sam, and he helped teach them to play guitar and bass, as Leon recalled it. He also later played drums with the group.

"We liked the Estrada Brothers, which was a Spanish band, and we became good friends with them and they would invite us," Leon said. "They had a Spanish hall over on Juarez Street. That is over by where the old Spudder ballpark used to be. We would go over there and we would listen to these guys play and we learned several Spanish songs we used all through the years."

The music had a Mexican flavor to it, even when many of the songs were supposed to be strictly country. The Spanish beat found its way into later hits by the Miller Brothers, undoubtedly traceable to that early friendship.

Leon picked up most of the music the brothers played, though, by listening to KWFT, a Wichita Falls station that carried both live and canned country music, and before long he and Nat and Sam began to wonder whether they were good enough to get a spot on the dial.

"We kept hearing these guys playing on the station, and we would go where they were playing sometimes and listen to them over the air," Leon said. In those days, bands would play live right in a radio station's own studios or the microphones and transmitting gear would be hauled right to the live venue by the station's crew.

"You know they had a room where you could come and watch through a window, and Joe Carrigan (who ran the radio station), Sam went to him and talked to him and asked him, would he come listen to us," Leon said. He said, "'No', but that if we would come down and try out he would listen to us at the station. So we went down and played for him and showed him a bunch of stuff where we had been playing and told him to ask Lefty Robertson and George Taylor and Dr. Kimbrough about us, and he said, 'Well, you boys can come on at a trial basis,' and this was all for free at first."

The boys didn't exactly get a spot during prime time. Their live show was broadcast from 6 a.m. to 6:30 a.m. every weekday morning. It was called The Gibbs Brothers.

Before long, the boys went from playing for free on the radio to playing for money with a real sponsor. Purina decided to take a chance on the boys, and ran a contest offering to give photographs away free through spots placed in the 6-6:30 program. If the give-away netted 500 photos, the boys would have a sponsor, and they did, in fact, account for that many to be handed out.

The sponsorship put the boys into what Leon laughingly refers to as "the big money." They were making $1 apiece for each program. That was $15 a week in the heart of the Depression.

"You could buy groceries for $3," Leon said.

They banked the money, which helped their

mother meet her bills and also helped her to move to progressively better houses over time.

The radio job led to other paying jobs, and before long the Gibbs Brothers were also playing square dances, among other things, all for money.

The square dances, Leon recalled, were on Friday and Saturday nights.

"This was hard work, my friend," he said. "Some dances would last seven minutes, maybe 10, while they called them. We were pretty successful with this because the guy hummed in a key and we would play the hoe-down to blend with his voice and we got kind of used to these callers and they thought that we were doing really good."

In 1936, the boys got a pretty good break.

Chevrolet and its local dealership were sponsoring a talent contest, with the local competition at the Majestic Theater in Wichita Falls. The Gibbs Brothers won first place.

Not long after that, the boys went with the local Chevy dealer to Dallas to continue in the competition at the Melba Theater.

"We stayed in the Baker Hotel in Dallas," Leon said. All expenses paid. Eat anything you want to. Sign your name.

"When we got on that stage at the Melba Theater, oh, you were looking at one scared boy or, I imagine, three. That booger had two balconies. The top one stuck out way over the middle, and the people were just right there in your face."

Of course, the boys had played up-close and personal before, but never to such a large crowd.

Before the show, Leon was grilled by the emcee, who had to try to fit commercial spots for Chevrolet into the lineup, about the price of a new master deluxe Chevy with everything on it. When Leon said he didn't know, the man gave him the answer he was to repeat back while on stage: $727. Dutifully, that was exactly the amount he gave on stage, and while he questioned in his own mind whether playing along was the right thing to do, he did so because he wanted so badly to perform and win.

The boys played "Under the Double Eagle," among other things, "and, honestly, people loved us, or they made like they did," Leon said.

They must have. The brothers won first place and a chance to return a month later to the same theater for the statewide contest.

They won third in that competition.

By this point, the Gibbs Brothers were playing for money every morning on their own radio program, were playing for dances at various locations around town, and were playing Sunday mornings at the Boys Club and Sunday evenings at the Pentecostal church they had joined as founding members years before.

They were looking to these contests to help them make a wider name for themselves and, of course, to make more money. Nothing, though, actually developed out of the Chevrolet-sponsored competitions.

Not long after, the brothers heard about a similar amateur contest that was to be conducted at the Pavilion on Lake Wichita featuring Wayne Raney, who Leon remembered as being billed as the world's greatest harmonica player, as emcee.

"We had to play because this guy was known worldwide," Leon said. "Honest, they billed him as the world's greatest harmonica player. He came to Wichita and he was the emcee of this contest at the lake and we were wanting to learn from him. We learned from everybody, because we were interested. We were truly doing what we truly loved and we loved every minute of it."

But the boys ran into a problem.

While practicing backstage with Wayne Raney, who was impressed with their abilities, they were interrupted.

"This guy walked up," Leon recalled. "I would give anything in the world if I knew who he was, I would shake his hand right now. He said, 'Sorry, boys, you guys are not going to be able to play in this thing. You are not amateur.' I did not know what he meant. Shoot, I had not heard of an amateur pro or what have you. He said there are a lot of people in this contest saying you all played for money and you are pros."

So instead of competing, the boys volunteered to be part of the program, and they stayed the night, playing without pay or hopes of winning anything.

"After we got through this deal, me, Sam and Nat had a meeting," Leon said. "Like somebody who had some sense, I said, 'Sam, we are not amateurs anymore. We do not play for any more Rotary Clubs, Lions Clubs. We don't play for nobody free, and you are the one that is going to get the money.'

"He said, 'Well, I don't know how much to ask for'."

"I said, 'Well, we will learn real fast. We will play for churches, but we don't play for anything else free.' So we upped our price. We had been playing Scotland, Texas, at the K of C Hall, and we upped our price to $3 apiece and $1 for the car, and we got it. They paid us. We upped our price everywhere we went, and they paid it, and it just started falling into place for us."

CHAPTER 5

B y the mid-1930s, Leon and Nat and Sam were musical pros, but they were also pros in the nonmusical world of work.

All three had paper routes with the Wichita Falls Record News and Times, owned and operated by Publisher/Editor Rhea Howard.

That meant they threw papers twice a day, since the *Record News* was the morning paper and the *Times* was the afternoon paper, both printed at the same plant but with different editorial staffs.

The boys had to get out of bed early every day of the week.

"We would get up at 3 a.m., make a paper route," Leon said. "Nat, Sam ... all three of us had to take routes then and get up there (to the radio station) about 20 or 30 minutes early for the radio program and play the radio program from 6 to 6:30, go home, eat breakfast, and leave for school at 8 a.m."

In addition to throwing two routes and going to school, they also worked on Saturday nights helping put sections of the paper together, a process called "inserting."

The task started about 8 p.m. with papers that had to get into the mail. That would take about two hours. Then there would be a break until about 10:30 p.m., when the inserters would get busy again. After midnight until about 3 a.m., the press was rolling and the inserters hurried to keep up with the press run.

"We delivered the paper in the evening from about 4 to 6, we played at night, we inserted, and then we threw our paper route in the morning," Leon said.

When did you find time to sleep?

"I do not know how we did it," he said. "But we did it."

About this same period in the mid-1930s, Nat went to work in the press room, and not long thereafter both Nat and Sam went to work in the advertising department of the newspaper.

Meanwhile, they continued to expand their musical horizons. Nat and Sam both took lessons at the Jack Kekunah Hawaiian School of Music, while Leon played with Kekunah and learned a lot from him, as well, he said.

Leon, Nat and Sam also played with Chuck Collins' Orchestra, and Collins taught Nat and Sam how to read music.

"He would hire them, and I would play a lot of jobs with them," Leon said. "But the minute I got on his bandstand people started requesting Western stuff, which did not help me too much with Chuck Collins, but it really helped Nat and Sam."

The Collins gig led to a brief collaboration by the boys with Frank Gordon and the Blue Jackets, who regularly played at a honky-tonk on Iowa Park Road called O.C. Glenn's Tavern. The boys had their own blue jackets with their names embroidered on them. Frank played banjo, Lee Cochran played trumpet, and the boys played their own instruments.

At about the same time, the boys were all three dating girls from the Pentecostal church they'd joined as founding members. Sam's girlfriend was Marvel Wise, and Nat's was Blanche Perkins, and Leon was dating Cleo Vaughn.

At age 17, Leon married Cleo.

The two ran away to Walters, Okla., for the ceremony, and returned to a hostile Mrs. Gibbs, who believed the two were too young and immature to be married. At first she refused to have anything to do with the couple, who had moved into their own place. Two weeks passed, and Leon went by to see his mother. Something had changed. "And she met me with open arms."

Leon and Cleo had moved into a small garage apartment on Indiana Street near Taylor Foundry that cost them $20 a month to rent.

Leon told the brothers he would need to find more music jobs so he could afford his new lifestyle. On one of those first grocery visits after the marriage — during which he bought sugar, salt, pepper, lard — what you'd need to outfit a kitchen with everything you'd need to cook from scratch – the total bill came to $3.27, a princely sum in those days. In today's dollars, that would be more than $42 (NewsEngin.com).

Shortly after the marriage, the Gibbs Brothers were recruited by Warren Silver and Bill Hood to come to KFDX radio to do a live program at 6:30 aIVVIVVIVV.m. every weekday morning from studios atop the City National Bank Building. The band at this point was comprised of the Gibbs brothers with Lee Cochran on trumpet, Bob Steed on drums and Tommy Bruce on lead guitar.

Leon laughed when he related the warning he got from Bill Hood about the program: "He would say, 'Now, men, this gets rough. We are going to start out with a 6:30 radio program in the morning. This gets rough and they expect you to be here. You must be here. Now, this is tough, and I want you boys to have it if you want it, but I want to tell you it's tough.'" Not too tough, though, on a crew that was already accustomed to getting up to throw papers at 3 a.m. every day.

At the time, the band was the only live program on KFDX, and the show was sponsored by a car dealership, among others. In fact, there were so many announcements that the boys could play no more than a half-dozen songs. But more than the money they earned for the live program, the boys wanted the show so they could make their own announcements about where they were going to be appearing, thus swelling the crowd for their shows. In addition, the band played dances in area towns, as well as weddings.

"At a wedding dance, we always played 'I Love You Truly,' and the second song was always at the request of the bride and groom," Leon said. "I don't ever remember us not knowing a song that was requested." He kept count, though, and recalled that more than 500 songs were asked for in that manner.

As their popularity grew, more of the people they ran into encouraged them to move back to KWFT, where there were a number of live country shows on the air.

Some of the programs on KWFT included the Callahan Brothers, the Cook Sisters Trio who sang gospel, Lillie Mae Comenski, the Harrington Sisters, the Stamps Baxter Quartet, Pop Stover and the Crazy Water Crystal Gang, and many others.

Another key reason for moving back to KWFT, Leon said, was its radio signal, which was beamed all the way into Kansas, a distance much greater than the signal sent by KFDX.

"We were traveling up in that direction, and more people could hear it up there," Leon said.

Meanwhile, Tommy Bruce and Bob Steed had had enough of playing almost every night and left the band about the time the boys were making their move back to KWFT.

Pete Martinez, who played steel guitar, joined the band for the move, as did J.E. Gose. The change gave the Gibbs Brothers more exposure, plus another big change.

In addition to playing in the band, Nat and Sam

Mike Whatley as partners.

First, though, Les and Mike persuaded the group to cut a record, with Les and Mike forming a record label, Delta Records, to handle the finances and sales. The band hired Jay Starnes as a vocalist, and Leon recalled that Jay had a stuttering problem when he talked but could sing "as clear as a bell."

"People loved him, they just didn't like to talk to him," Leon said.

Les and Mike booked a recording studio in Dallas to make the first Miller Brothers album.

Three of the songs on the record were written by Jay Starnes – "My Baby Girl," "Shadows On My Memory" and "Bluest Blues." Leon played a fiddle tune called "Wednesday Night Waltz" and another called "Shanty Town," which had the band all singing in unison.

No one can remember how, exactly, the record was marketed, but it sold well, according to Leon:

Naturally, Pauline at Tanner's store, she really sold these things, and I thought Mr. Tanner would get upset about this with me working there, but he said, "No, I've met a lot of new people here because of this," and she ordered and reordered and reordered these things and they sold real good for us. And Mr. Tanner would even run an ad in the paper telling about Miller Brothers recordings, and it didn't cost us a penny.

Almost immediately thereafter, the brothers joined with Les Fulcher and Mike Whatley to play at Les and Mike's club downtown over the old Wichita Falls *Post* newspaper building, right off Scott Street and one block from the Marchman Hotel on 10th and Travis.

Before the war, the enforcement of city codes on maximum numbers of occupants in a public building was lax. Leon recalled that you could sell as many tickets to an event in a club as you could print, and the customers were happy to be standing if there were no tables available. But at some point the law had changed, and each building had a maximum occupancy. A sign noting that maximum number had to be posted in clear view. "We had large crowds," Leon said, "and it's pretty hard to turn people away who are trying to buy a ticket. Sometimes I felt like we were oversold at the door. The parking got to be a problem. Many customers would park in the Marchman Hotel's street parking space. This didn't go well, I'm sure, and last but not least Saturday night was the night that the *Post* printed the newspaper all night to get that big Sunday paper ready, and all of these things plus some might get a little loud from maybe a little too much to drink" – all this led to a decision on the part of the boys to leave that club and find something else.

Another band was abandoning its locale, so the boys took up the lease on a building at 705 Travis that had been home to the 400 Club run by Billy Peeler. They put a big neon sign out front with *Miller Brothers Club* in lights.

The band played Thursday and Saturday nights, and added some personnel. Freddie Navarte joined as a sax player, Clyde Smith joined on sax and clarinet, and Lee Cochran joined as a trumpet player and singer.

"We had an eight-piece band that could play anything from rumbas, sambas, tangos, the latest hit songs in all the country, and Western Swing — all the country songs from the oldest to the newest," Leon said.

Over the course of the next year or so, the band's personnel changed. Jay Starnes died, and Pauline had to leave because it appeared that the group was going to do more road work away from home. Madge Suttee took her place at the piano, and Leon said she was one of the best piano players in the business. Dewayne Bass signed on to sing – "and sing, man, that kid could sing." Bass also played steel guitar.

The band was consistently playing to sell-out crowds, and the boys figured out why. The more country their music was, the earlier people would get there to dance because soon there were no seats left.

To a lot of folks in those days, country meant Western Swing, the creation and popularizaton of which has been traced to fellow Texas musician Bob Wills.

Actually, at some point prior to their service in the military, the boys had gotten an inkling that if they could play like Bob Wills and his Texas Playboys, they might make more money. And with their own club, they went in that direction more intensely than before.

Western Swing had been part of their repertoire even in the 1930s, mainly because of the popularity of the genre in the Texas towns where they played:

> Public dancing became, by the 1930s, one of the key American courtship rituals. For many young people, swing music and dancing served as important emotional outlets; for others, they offered much-needed escape from the economic difficulties of the lingering Depression. With partner in hand, caught up in shared euphoria and momentary forgetfulness, dancers could stomp and swing themselves into states of transcendence. While the music's time surged forward, real-world time, paradoxically, seemed to stop. … If ballrooms had won public acceptance in the 1920s and offered a diversion from the Depression of the early 1930s, in the late thirties they reached their all-time center stage in American youth culture, just as rock and roll would two decades later. (*Jazz: The First Century* 56)

People also knew what they liked because the radio had become a ubiquitous instrument, available in virtually every home. Records were increasingly less and less expensive to listen to at home as well.

"By 1938, approximately 82 percent of U.S. households had a radio. ... By the dawn of the television era in the early 1950s, more than 2,500 radio stations were broadcasting into the nation's homes" (*The Century Begins* 38).

> Throughout the nation, swelling masses of listeners and dancers created an explosion in the popularity of jukeboxes, on which swing recordings were increasingly heard. The number of jukeboxes in the United States jumped dramatically from 25,000 in 1933 to 300,000 in 1939, by then consuming 13 million discs a year. Spurred on by the swing-music craze, the recovering economy, the popularity of the phonograph, the jukebox boom, and the new low-priced (35-cent) discs issued by music-industry upstart Decca Records and others, the record industry climbed back to recovery. From a low of 10 million units sold in 1933, sales surged to 33 million in 1938 and 127 million in 1941. (*Jazz: The First Century* 56)

Apparently, though, swing bands began to die out during the war years, and only a few big bands remained at the war's end (*The Swing Age* 276).

But there was no dying out of interest in the likes of Bob Wills, who had at least a decade of fame behind him in the mid-1940s, and that, along with the continued strong demand for it, is what kept the Gibbs brothers interested in the music.

After the war, Wills' music changed, too. He adapted a style that was right in line with what The Miller Brothers were emphasizing – lots of strings. The use of plenty of strings actually allowed Wills to cut back on his band personnel without affecting the quality of his music.

"At public appearances fans always required the fiddle tunes that helped make Wills famous, and he therefore began to feature his own fiddle more. Wills was so popular after the war that he could get along without the large bands and orchestras he used when he was building his reputation in the 1930s" (*San Antonio Rose* 238).

Leon and the brothers could not have ignored Wills' influence even if they'd wanted to:

> In the postwar years, success came to Wills and his Texas Playboys at every turn. Nearly every record they cut was a hit or at least sold out in most shops. When Wills could not provide enough new recordings to satisfy the demand, Columbia decided to reissue some of his prewar material originally released on Vocalion as far back as 1935. In a single year, 1947, Columbia reissued 70 Bob Wills recordings, and many of these sold better than when they were first issued. Thousands came to his dances; in many instances attendance records were broken and people were turned away. The famous swing orchestras in California discovered that many of their followers were leaving to dance to Bob Wills's Western Swing. (*San Antonio Rose* 239)

When the Miller Brothers played songs from the Wills repertoire, they would generally do the tunes exactly as they could be heard on radio or on a phonograph record. "Actually, when we played their songs, we played them exactly like they played them – Hank Thompson or anybody," Leon said. "If we had a request for their song, people wanted to hear – say, 'Faded Love' – they wanted to hear that song."

That's the way the band approached popular music, but that's not the way the group approached the songs they had written themselves or older tunes. On those, Leon said they "had to jazz it up."

When we played the simplest little old tunes we copied from some big band, a simple song like 'Little Brown Jug,' man, we had a knock-down intro on that thing that everybody loved. Then we went into 'Little Brown Jug' just as simple as it was written. Where we did most of our improvising, was on intros and when you give the trumpet man a chord or the piano man a chord – or the fiddle man. Anybody is going to jazz it up. But, as far as really inventing or coming out with something new, we didn't. In other words, when they give you a chord you are going to invent something because you are … you are just playing stuff in that chord progression.

So popular was country and Western Swing in Wichita Falls, The Miller Brothers Club soon opened on other nights than Thursday-Saturday so other bands could be booked to play.

Leon remembered booking Hank Laughlin and John Lee Wills, who was Bob's brother, early on.

Before long, it became clear to the three brothers that there was money to be made not only in playing a couple of nights a week with their own band but also in booking other bands in the Wichita Falls club and elsewhere, too.

And that's about the time the Miller Brothers got down to just one "Miller."

CHAPTER 8

During the relatively short period of time the Miller Brothers had their club open at 705 Travis, they underwent some major changes in direction – not musically, but personally.

Sam had been the financial manager of the organization, and in 1947 or '48, he saw an opportunity to branch out. Together with Nat and Leon, he and Lee Cochran, their trumpet player, put together a booking agency for other bands.

Sam quit the band and began running the agency out of his home and started booking the 10 or 12 bands that made their home base Wichita Falls. That included a black band called Doc Jones, among others.

His move was that of a visionary, and Sam was ahead of his time in seeing a need and filling it.

With Sam's agency, "Regional dance venues began getting quality, pre-screened groups on a regular, dependable basis; groups didn't have to spend so much of their time just hustling for jobs; calendars could become standardized across the region, almost forming a smaller version of the old vaudeville circuits," according to musician, music critic and historian Don Chance of Dallas.

Before long, the agency was handling 50 bands or more, booking them into various clubs and gigs around the country and even helping out when other agencies failed to carry through with a deal. Leon remembered, for example, one such gig when Tex Ritter had been booked into a dance in Olney, Texas, but his band members had been, by mistake, booked into a dance someplace else. It just so happened that The Miller Brothers

Band was not booked and agreed to the money Tex Ritter offered. Leon said, though, that they might have gone anyway just to be able to say they'd played with the famous movie and music star.

Sam's ability to get along with bands and club owners kept his clientele growing, and he became well-known and respected throughout the industry.

Pretty soon, Chance said, he expanded his business to the extent that his Sam Gibbs Orchestra Service groups were working regularly in almost every part of the United States. "Not content to just operate domestically, he built up his military contacts and started booking groups at bases around the world. Never before in American musical entertainment history had a single booking agency controlled such a vast territory. Though most other agents would eventually copy his networking methods and attention to detail, some even more successfully, Sam Gibbs can legitimately claim credit for virtually inventing the casual live entertainment booking industry."

Over time, as Sam's influence grew so did good-humored speculation about how he went about doing what he did. Some began jokingly calling him "Dartboard Sam," based on the notion that he liked to close his eyes and throw a dart at a large map of the country or the world and wherever the dart stuck, the band whose booking schedule he was working on at the time would play there next, no matter how far away it might be.

"The actual truth of the matter is a bit more complicated," Chance explained. "Though Sam worked very carefully routing his groups, trying to make sure everyone he had out on the road moved smoothly from job to job at the same time and with distances between bookings as short as possible, problems always seemed to come up. Often, most often, these problems would come from the bands themselves."

Family problems, interpersonal disagreements, alcohol abuse – all kinds of problems could crop up on a tour. And then there were highway accidents, gear malfunctions that kept groups from meeting the demands of their schedule. As time passed, though, Sam realized he wouldn't always be able to book bands for a living. He realized that over time the entertainment business would change, and the many small regional groups would eventually settle into "home" clubs or the genre would cease to exist as it had during the 50s and 60s. Groups were becoming increasingly expensive to book, and crowd tastes were splintering. So he began to look for something else.

Sam started a small accessory store supplying strings and other items for his musicians. But before long that part of his business was really growing, and eventually he opened a 9,000-square-foot music store, which carried a full line of instruments and featured a repair shop and teaching studios.

In a 1980 interview published in the *Wichita Falls Record News*, Sam told reporter Jo Thornley Cox that he traveled hundreds of thousands of miles as a booking agent. "I've traveled as much as 97,000 miles a year in the car," he said. "That's not counting the plane trips."

At the time of the '80 interview, Sam was booking 37 bands, mostly in the country and western field but with some rock, disco and R&B thrown in. The "meat" of the agency, he said, was wrapped in the road musicians. He took care in making sure that they were treated right. "If a fellow is in school, I won't let him go on the road," he said. "Education's real important." Not that you couldn't learn from being on the road. "Nothing's greater for a musician – if he doesn't do it too long – just to enjoy seeing the scenery. And you meet a lot of people."

Acknowledging what he had come to understand

about the toll that being on the road too long can take, he added: "Road groups will work six nights. This is their livelihood, and they don't have a home. They're a different breed of person from the guy who wants to play only weekends. We call them the Weekend Warriors" (*Times Record News,* Aug. 8, 1980: 1B).

Undoubtedly, Sam's most famous band was Bob Wills and The Texas Playboys.

Leon remembered when Bob called Sam about joining the agency and Sam went to Tulsa to talk to the then-world-renowned band leader. He remembered that in a lot of ways Bob was a hard man to deal with, even when he wasn't drinking.

For example, on tour, bands were expected to work seven days a week, a schedule Bob protested.

One day, Leon said, Bob called Sam to complain and to tell Sam that from then on Sundays were an off day for Bob. Sam agreed, but he also took out his schedule book for the Texas Playboys and wrote Bob a letter.

"I saw the letter Sam wrote Bob," Leon said. It said, "Bob, I know you're tired because I figured out with your 40-minute shows you worked a little over 10 hours this month."

Sam booked Wills for 18 years.

Eventually, Sam stopped booking bands altogether and devoted his time to the music store, which continues in operation on Jacksboro Highway in Wichita Falls. "Though Sam Gibbs Orchestra Service ceased operations in the mid-1980s, many of the booking practices and policies Sam developed over a half-century ago were an industry-wide standard for many years," Chance said.

While all the travel and pressure of booking entertainers undoubtedly took their toll on Sam's family life, that's not the way his daughter Paula Moore remembered things.

"He loved to fish and while not necessarily a good fisherman, along with his sons-in-law, he fished the Montana River for paddle fish, and took deep-sea fishing trips with all his daughters and their families," said Paula. "He was a great family man and hunted year after year with grandsons and sons-in-law. The entire families would camp out and make a fun outing for all." In addition, Sam loved to read, and much of what he read he would draw on in speeches to various groups.

After retiring, Sam and his wife Marvel spent time traveling with friends, and bought a retirement home in Zapata, Texas.

"While living in Zapata, he enjoyed gardening, a little fishing, but mostly relaxing," Paula said. "He did volunteer work with the Adult Literacy Council, teaching adults to read and write. One small rancher was unable to even write his name. He also taught Spanish to Winter Texans (those from more northern states who spent their winters in the warmth of the Gulf coast region). Along with a group of men from his church he was able to help them obtain a charter for a Rotary club. He volunteered also with the Zapata Library and served on their board to raise funds for new books."

As Sam and Marvel aged, they developed severe health problems that prompted them to move back to Wichita Falls to be closer to family.

"He was strong and disciplined in all aspects of his life," Paula said. "They (the boys) had started work at such a young age, and had known from the beginning they had to take care of their mother and younger sister. They knew even then what it would take to survive in those difficult times. They each had a very good work ethic."

While thinking of her dad, Paula recalled the times they would travel, him on business and everyone else on an outing. She also talked about her intense love for the man.

In 1949, Nat also decided it was time for a change in his own personal direction. The music schedule, with some out-of-town trips thrown in along with trying to run the wholesale drug business, was just too much.

Was it a hard decision to leave the band?

"Well, if I hadn't been hen-pecked I guess it would have been," Nat recalled. "My wife said, 'OK, we have two boys, and I'm not going to raise these two boys by myself.'" Nat noted that Sam and Leon also had children. They had girls. His wife responded, "Well, they can have the girls. I've got to raise these boys. I wish you'd just find something else.'

"All along, even with the drug store, I was looking for other things."

This time, the "other thing" turned out to be an advertising sales job at the *Dallas Times Herald*, and a virtually complete break from the music world.

As he had done before with all his other jobs, he threw himself into his work in Dallas.

"When I started to go to the *Dallas Times Herald*, I told Sam, and Sam said, 'Oh, crap.' He said, 'That's the big city, and there's so many people down there, you are going to be fighting against so many people. Aren't you a little worried about going down there in that atmosphere?' And, I said, 'No, I'm not. Because I think I know what I'm doing.'" Nat smiled as he told the story. "So, when I got down there, after about three or four months, I said to Sam, 'If you can make it in a small town, man, you've got it made in a big town. They don't know how to work. They don't know how to work.' And that's how I found it. Lots of nice people, lots of good people. But people don't work like you had to work at the *Times*."

For eight years, Nat worked at the *Times Herald* in the ad sales department, and at every opportunity he took on more responsibility.

He said he more fully developed there some of the talents and skills he'd been working on for years ever since he was a kid – developing good work habits and learning not only how to work for other people but how to be their boss. "In short, I learned the reason for doing right today is tomorrow," he said.

Nat made a rapid rise at the newspaper and was happy there, but he felt, he said, that he still had room to grow. Then one day the salesman in charge of the Affiliated Food Stores account called in sick, and Nat filled in for him to make a sales call to the cooperative food giant based in Dallas.

"As I was walking down the hall, the CEO of Affiliated saw me and asked me to come into his office," he recalled. "He closed the door and said, 'I want to hire you as advertising director.' Now, I didn't tell him but my price when thinking of changing jobs was twice my present salary. He offered me three times my salary plus a bonus each year of one-fortieth of 1 percent for each $1 million sales increase the company made. With the bonus, the first year I made five times my previous salary."

Over the next eight years, Affiliated stores saw their sales go from $22 million in 1957 to $137.7 million in 1964.

In '64 while still with Affiliated, Nat organized and developed the Nat Gibbs Advertising, Inc., with clients in Texas, Oklahoma, Arkansas and Louisiana. Not long after that, he was enticed to fold the agency to help Associated Wholesale Grocers of Little Rock get out of business trouble.

Then trouble developed at Affiliated in Dallas, and Nat was asked to return as chairman of the board and chief executive officer. He was given a five-year contract, but he saw it renewed several times over.

Nat was an organizer, a hard-worker and a visionary when it came to the business world.

Affiliated was a kind of privately run grocery co-operative, allowing stockholding members to buy products in bulk, thus saving money, so they could compete against the large grocery chains. In addition to consolidating that buying power, Affiliated also had warehouse space to keep food in bulk and its own fleet of trucks to move products wherever they needed to go.

Immediately after taking over at Affiliated, he initiated an aggressive buying program, put together a hard-hitting ad program for all media, bought a printing press to consolidate publication of grocery circulars and other ad materials, and began pushing Shurfine, a private label unavailable to stores outside the Affiliated family.

In addition, member stores needed help on merchandising and on planning and implementing growth strategies, and under Nat's direction Affiliated began providing those services plus a lending program to help members come up with the money they needed to expand.

He developed a construction company to build retail grocery stores, oversaw development of an accounting program for retailers and established two insurance entities to serve stock holders.

Before long, Nat was chairman of the board of Shurfine Central in Chicago, at the time the sixth largest Chicago-based company.

When he was 61, he started trying to retire, but the board wouldn't hear of it. Instead, they gave him a contract to work just two days a month, for $200,000 a year.

He and his wife Blanche bought a ranch in Mount Vernon, Texas, and Nat pursued real estate deals in the Dallas area, including one that involved buying 68 acres in Southlake for $154,000 and then selling it some time later for $2.1 million.

In 1987, he retired for good, but remained active in the First Baptist Church of Mount Vernon and in various business and charitable organizations.

As for music, after Nat left Wichita Falls he picked up the sax and learned to play it and tried to play occasionally with a group in Dallas. But, eventually, he found he enjoyed just playing for his own pleasure.

Looking back at a hugely successful career, Nat said he found only a couple of reasons for it.

First: "Hard work. I never asked anyone to do anything I couldn't. If I can't do it better I don't want to make someone do better."

Second: "Many nights when we three boys were small I heard my mother pray for the Lord to watch over and take care of her boys. I know God was not only watching and taking care of me then, but throughout my life. So I can't be proud at heart because I give God the credit for anything that has been accomplished in my life."

were still selling advertising for the Times Publishing Co., and Leon was throwing a very long paper route twice a day and inserting at night when he could.

One day, Joe Carrigan, who ran KWFT, was in the *Times* offices visiting with Rhea Howard when Sam Gibbs, Leon said, walked into the building. "There's one of my men right now," Joe Carrigan said. "No, that's one of the Gibbs boys, and they all three have been with me all their life, I guess, since they were kids," Rhea Howard told him.

Not long after that, Howard called the brothers to his office and told them: "Fellows, it is not treating Joe Carrigan right, and it is not treating me right. You cannot work for two advertising companies."

Sam spoke right up, as Leon remembered it, and told Howard how appreciative the brothers were for their jobs and all that he had done for them, then promised the boys would stay with the *Times*.

Soon after that the boys went to Carrigan, who told them, "You boys are doing too good with music to quit it now." He suggested they simply change their name to Jones or Smith, maybe Miller Brothers or something. They agreed on the spot. They were now The Miller Brothers, the name they went by from then on.

The music, however, was the same, and its popularity was growing.

In addition to having their own show on the radio, the boys also played backup with Pop Stover, who had a musical variety/comedy half-hour program the boys would later mimic, to a degree, in their own professional road show. They had another set of new names, too, for the Stover program. Leon was Junior Stover, Sam was Buford, and Nat was Kokomo. Together, they did impromptu skits and played songs without any rehearsal whatsoever. The experience proved important. Their work on the program helped set the stage for a popular part of the regular program the Miller Brothers put together when they went on the road after returning from World War II.

Increasingly, the band was playing out of town for weddings or dances.

"This situation was great for all five of us," Leon said. "We took out expenses, gas or anything we needed for a particular job and split the money five ways. It got bigger and better all the time."

In 1939, Sam married Marvel Wise and Nat married Blanche Perkins, but they didn't have much time to spend with their brides because that was also the year that the group decided to schedule and sponsor their own Saturday night dance. They booked the Woodmen of the World Hall above Hub Clothiers in downtown Wichita Falls. Almost immediately, the crowds got so large that the boys had to move. The authorities were afraid the floor would cave in.

They quickly found another place: 812 Scott St. downtown, across from the Strand Theater and just down the street from the City National Bank building. The boys laid the wood floor themselves, and they almost failed to have it finished in time for their big opening night, which they had already announced many times in their radio program.

The doors were to open at 7:30 p.m., but the boys didn't finish their work on the place until 7. They ran home to clean up and get into their outfits, and sent their wives back to the club to start selling tickets. The boys had been afraid nobody would show up. Instead they had a full house. Even though they did not sell alcoholic beverages, the capacity Saturday night crowds turned out to be normal.

Bill Sharp, an announcer from KWFT, would come to the front door every Saturday night after the band had started playing, and he would find out from the ticket-taker how big the crowd was. Then he would go back to the station and announce that, say, 920 people were enjoying the music and ask everyone in his audience to join the fun.

"A thousand was a good crowd," Leon recalled. "When we hit 1,000 we were real happy. And we had just jumped the price up to 60 cents for men, 40 cents for ladies. Now this may sound stupid, but it worked: We always, always, saw that we were a little bit higher than anybody else. I kept telling the guys – it would scare them – hey, that automatically makes you the best or you couldn't get it. We always did this. Later on at the M-B Corral we did it. Not much, but just so we were higher."

By 1940, with the rumors of war reaching Wichita Falls, the Miller Brothers were booked as many as six nights a week.

They counted themselves among the lucky, because Wichita Falls, while it had grown by about 1,300 people during the 30s, was still in the thrall of the Depression as the new decade began.

At Christmas 1938, for example, nearly 3,000 children were approved to receive toys from the Advertising Club's seasonal relief drive. At the same time, 800 families were certified as qualifying to receive Salvation Army Christmas baskets, but the Army had planned for only 600 families (50th anniversary issue). In 1940, the City Council approved a new food stamp program for the needy, and put up $6,000 to get into the program.

The prospect of war was getting closer and closer to home as the new decade got under way, and with it came the prospect of prosperity.

In November 1940, Maj. Gen. Rush B. Lincoln, commandant of the Army-Air Corps technical schools, met with two dozen businessmen and within two weeks had an offer of $75,000 and land for an air base in Wichita

Falls. Construction started in 1941, the year of Pearl Harbor.

With the new decade, things changed significantly in the band, as well. Nat Gibbs left the group in 1940 to focus on his job at the newspaper and his new family.

The band was not enough for the boys anymore anyway. In 1942, the three of them bought a drugstore, the Lamar Street Pharmacy, mainly because it was for sale and because Nat had always had a hankering to be a pharmacist. Nat left the advertising business to run the drugstore.

"Because of war wage - price controls at that time, many items were in short supply," Nat remembered. "But we found ways to stay ahead by improvising. We purchased ice cream mix from dairies and manufactured ice cream ourselves. Each month we showed a healthy increase in sales and profit and were very comfortable in our new environment ..." (Nat's handwritten biography).

Not long after, though, Nat and Sam were drafted. They went into the Navy and served together aboard ship, an oddity at the time because the military had an official policy that brothers shouldn't be put in harm's way. Then it was Leon's turn.

CHAPTER 6

In late 1944, after his brothers Nat and Sam had already gone through Naval basic training and were serving aboard the same ship, Leon was drafted into the Army and went to Dallas for his physical exam, then on to Fort Wolters at Mineral Wells, Texas, for basic training.

He found the regimen to be tough. He was, after all, nearly 22, much older than the average draftee, a teenager.

But he also found his way into a musical gig.

One of the sergeants in charge of his training unit found out that Leon and another draftee from Wichita Falls named Gerald Jones could play musical instruments. One night, he had heard them singing and playing in the barracks. So the sergeant asked them to play for a party downtown, which they did, and after that they had no trouble getting passes into town to play regularly at clubs.

Leon could make $5 for a Saturday night, which he did many times. Some weekends, though, he tried hitchhiking back to Wichita Falls to see his wife and daughter. Eventually, he was able to get an apartment in Mineral Wells so the family could all be together. Not for long, though. Two weeks before his training ended, Cleo and the daughter went back to Wichita Falls, and Leon joined them for a few days after graduating.

During that break before taking his first assignment, Leon went back to the Miller Brothers Hall for one more dance.

"Pete and J.E.," he said, "were still there with a bunch of guys I didn't know." He said he stayed a few minutes and left. "But right after that, Pete and J.E. left too. I

43

don't know if the crowds held up or what happened to them."

Not that it mattered. Leon had worries of his own, because he was assigned as an infantryman in a war that was being won a foot at a time by soldiers moving across North Africa and from island to island in the South Pacific.

After his 10-day furlough, he joined his fellow infantry graduates in Dallas for a train trip to California where he had the dispiriting experience of learning to load and unload a duffel bag only to lose it forever once it was out of his sight.

With his musical background, why didn't Leon try to get into a military band or orchestra or some part of the Army that would provide entertainment services?

"I tried every day I was in the service," he said. "I tried to get into Special Services. I tried and tried and tried. It shows on my record that I was a musician."

Nevertheless, as far as the Army was concerned, Leon was a rifleman destined for service in the infantry.

Finally, in early 1945, the men boarded the USS Cape Henlopin for a destination unknown to them, other than that it would be in the South Pacific.

For 20 days, the men were on the ship and were joined by a dozen others before landing at Leyte, an island in the Philippines.

The men were to be replacements in F Company of the 164th Infantry in the American Division, which had already seen action in the region.

Much of the fighting in the Pacific was done by the U.S. Marines, but the Army also had a significant presence there, even at the outset of the war when Japan launched its surprise attack on Pearl Harbor in December of 1941.

In fact, to get to the resource-rich Dutch East Indies

the Japanese had to take the Philippines, wrestling control from green native troops led by Americans who were not very prepared themselves. In fact, right after Pearl Harbor, the Japanese had launched all-out attacks on Filipino-American forces (*World War II*—The Associated Press 52).

Because saving the Philippines was never part of the strategy of war-planners in Washington, the troops there were left without significant support, and eventually thousands of Americans were killed or captured (*World War II*— The AP 74).

In 1944, at the urging of Gen. Douglas MacArthur, who had grown up in the Philippines and helped build and train its armies, the Washington strategy changed to allow the U.S. Navy and U.S. troops to try to retake the islands. Hearing that Japanese forces were least resistant on Leyte, MacArthur took aim at this island that was about 100 miles long in the middle of the Philippine chain. In October, the fighting began, and MacArthur declared the battle for Leyte won on Dec. 26. But it wasn't. There was "mopping up" left to do, and that's what Leon and his buddies were heading into (*World War II* — AP 198-199).

They were taken to shore by Murphy boats, the kind familiar to Americans who have seen photos or movies depicting landings in France on D-Day. The boats move right up to shore, a gated door unhinges from the top, and the boat disgorges frightened troops, often into the tide, not onto the beach.

"When you got off they would warn you, 'Now, keep your rifle above your head, keep you some ammunition above your head, and keep your cigarettes above your head," Leon says. "Water was way up, just right to your neck. And here were all these guys and darn if I didn't forget about my cigarettes.

"As we finally got on shore, there wasn't any shooting at first, so we thought, man, we got this made," Leon recalled of that first day. The men got careless and, instead of moving through the jungle, they began following a trail that had been cut through the thick vegetation.

"As we were going down this road, we heard a shot," he said. "And everybody hit the dirt beside the path. There were several shots fired, but you could tell they were kind of way off, not real close. When we hit the dirt at the side of this path, wouldn't you know I landed in an ant bed. Black ants. I whispered to my old buddy, so he could hear me, 'Move over. I'm in an ant bed.' He asked if they were black, and I said, yes. They were black ants. I had never seen anything like this. So, I went up there, and he said, 'Well, there are some of them up here, too.'"

Fortunately, they didn't have to wait long before the sergeant had them moving again.

"As we moved out, there hung a Japanese, a Jap," Leon said. "He had tied himself to this tree, and no telling how many GIs had shot him, but he was still hanging." That was their welcome to Leyte.

The green replacements were not expecting to encounter anything worse, but the grunts, like Leon, knew little about their objective and the island itself, but they learned quickly from veterans, some of whom had been fighting on Leyte for months.

One of the first seasoned troops Leon ran into gave him some advice: "Don't be brave. Don't try to do anything stupid. When you hear a shot hit the ground. Look and try to see where it is coming from. And start shooting back. But don't try to be a hero. 'Cause heroes get killed first." Leon said the man then lit a cigarette. He put it up to his mouth, stopped, and said he'd been there two years. Again he tried to hit his mouth with the cigarette. He missed again. And again. "And I thought ... well ... I wasn't nervous like he was until later. Later that day."

The men started moving inland.

"We went on down this little path a little farther, and by this time it was about 5 o'clock in the evening and Lord help me if we didn't run into a bunch of fire," he said. "We weren't expecting all this," so they stopped and camped there that night.

Leon used his small GI-issue shovel to dig a deep enough indentation in the earth so he could hide most of his body. That first night on the island was miserable. Constant rifle fire around the perimeter the men had set up to protect themselves made sleep impossible.

Days and nights were spent going up and down one hill after another, chasing an elusive enemy and dodging the Japanese who were still around to fight.

"About the end of the first week, the BAR man got wounded and the sergeant asked who wanted the job. It automatically makes you a buck sergeant," Leon said. "No one stepped forward. No one. He looked at us and said, 'Gibbs, you're it.' I told him I didn't like the BAR in basic training and I did not even know how to clean it. I knew nothing about it. He threw it in my arms and said, 'You'd better learn it and learn quick.'"

Apparently, he did. The Browning Automatic Rifle was not as heavy or as difficult to operate as a .50-caliber machinegun, but it did weigh 18.5 pounds and was almost four feet long. The weapon shot .30-caliber rounds and had an effective range of 600 yards.

For weeks, Leon's outfit chased Japanese stragglers, until finally his part of the Americal Division was finished with Leyte.

It's been estimated that 70,000 Japanese troops fought on Leyte, and only 5,000 survived. Twenty-seven thousand of them died after the December declaration of victory by General MacArthur (*World War II* — AP 199).

Leaving Leyte, Leon and his company moved on

to Cebu, another island in the Philippines, an island no American troops had set foot on since the beginning of the war.

"It was the same thing as Leyte, only more enemy and more of them were dug in," Leon said. "After the LST got as close as they could, the prow dropped, and they were waiting for us — *ooh, ooh, spread out, men. Get to shore as quick as you can.* We did, but they were shooting all the time." The Americans were trying to get to where there were trees, so they could hide.

The fighting was heavier on Cebu than it had been on Leyte, and a man had to stay constantly alert, especially on night guard duty, which meant peering into the blackness for four hours and imagining the worst.

Leon said he was scared every minute of every night he spent on guard duty.

"You could see things that you swore were moving," he said. "You could see, and you'd wait and all of a sudden you could look around, look back, and it would be gone. And you could swear you saw something there. I shot many a tree all to pieces. That's no lie. I was always brought up in a Christian home and always believed in prayer, and still do. Anyway, every step you take when they are shooting at you, I would pray."

Still, through two islands' worth of fighting, Leon saw only a couple of men from his unit killed. Countless Japanese died, though, during his three months on Cebu.

After Cebu, they headed next to the island of Negros.

"This was a stronghold for the Japs," Leon said. "This one got tough and rough. We spent longer and longer when we took a hill, longer than we had before. We knew we were fighting a lot more people, and we got on top of a hill and we couldn't get off of it."

That was especially true of one mountain the unit

found itself trapped on for days. Day and night, "they would come at us with everything they had." Finally, the sergeant put together a squad of men that included Leon to try to find a safe way down the mountain. Instead, they found the key to their escape.

From one angle on the trail they could look up. "Right on top of the mountain where we'd been sleeping every night, there was this big cave." The men tossed dynamite into it and when the smoke cleared, they found a dozen dead Japanese, machineguns and stacks of ammunition.

It was on Negros not long after that when Leon came close to being killed in an ambush.

The squad of men he was with got caught in a crossfire.

"Man, we crawled, walking on our hands and knees, and we really fired the ammunition. And this BAR got real hot. And you talk about praying. This thing got hot as fire, and I grabbed it. The sergeant said, 'Get off here, get out of here.' I grabbed the steel part with my hands and I didn't know I had the thing for two or three minutes. We started crawling, getting away from there."

While Leon had escaped with his life, he did have a burn whose severity failed to make an impression on him at first, mainly because getting out of the ambush did not end the fighting. The Japanese were lobbing mortars into Leon's unit, and at least one of his buddies was killed.

More than one full day passed before it dawned on Leon that his right hand was really badly burned – "Man, that hand was so sore I couldn't move it — swollen and red and burned up, and red streaks going up my arm."

As soon as the reality of the situation set in, the first thing that crossed Leon's mind was how or whether he'd ever be able to play the fiddle again.

The medic took one look at the wound and said, "Get this man out of here. He's got an infection in this. Got blood poisoning."

Along with a half-dozen injured GIs, Leon went to a field hospital, where he was treated for a few days until major fighting in the highlands sent a large number of casualties to be treated. Since he was not fatally hurt, Leon was removed to a tent facility that was actually operated for Filipino fighters.

There, a physician that Leon figures was Chinese made a decision that most likely saved Leon's life.

"This Chinese doctor came in and said, told another guy … 'Send this man home where he belongs. We've doctored this here. If we cut this off out here it will never heal.'"

If the hand couldn't heal, it would probably have to be amputated, the doctor said.

Within a few hours, Leon found himself on an airplane with other wounded soldiers, landing for a fuel layover in Hawaii and then ultimately landing at Fort Bliss, Texas, where doctors operated on his hand.

"Everything came out OK," Leon said, flexing the fingers of his right hand, the one he has used for years to run the bow over the fiddle strings for thousands of listeners.

But it took several operations and months of treatment at military hospitals for everything to turn out well, and at times Leon wondered if his hand and fingers would ever be flexible enough to let him play again.

While at Fort Bliss, he heard that the Japanese had surrendered.

On leave to recuperate at home in Wichita Falls, Leon learned that his wife and daughter Carole were having a terrible time trying to make ends meet. A pastor even offered to send letters to the military expediting

Leon's discharge from the Army so he could make a little more than the $150 per month he was earning.

"And I said, 'I don't want to be a quitter, but I don't want to go back, truthfully. And the war is going to end, I feel like, real soon now.' So I said, 'If you could please help me in any way.'" And he did.

When Leon's discharge came through a short time later, he noticed that he was listed as a private, not a sergeant, which was the rank he'd been promoted to as a BAR man.

"But I didn't say anything. I wanted to come home." And in January 1946 that's what he did.

CHAPTER 7

W hen the Gibbs brothers came home from the war, having been among the 12,000 men and women who served from Wichita County, they found a Wichita Falls that was bursting at the seams.

At its peak, Sheppard Field, built north of the city just as the war was getting under way, had more than 46,000 troops, and many of them spilled over into the community. The base closed on Sept. 1, 1946, but the deactivation was not a huge blow because the city had been planning for its eventual closure (*Times Record News* 50th anniversary):

> The city had set up a planning and zoning commission and let the contract for the conduit to bring in Lake Kickapoo water. To bring in new industry and help expand existing plants, an industrial fund was created. Hardin Junior College became a senior college … Citizens supported an $800,000 bond issue to expand Wichita General Hospital, a $200,000 addition to Bethania Hospital was outlined, and the building fund of the YMCA passed $400,000 as construction began. More than two dozen churches announced building improvement programs totaling in excess of $1 million, including a new edifice for Fain Memorial Presbyterian Church. (*Times Record News* 50th anniversary)

Not long after, in 1947, the price of oil hit $2 per barrel for the first time since 1926, went on up to $2.65, and business optimism was further encouraged by a survey report that at least 1,000 new homes were needed to meet housing demands.

Wichita Falls was clearly taking part in the wild prosperity that came with the end of the war, as veterans settled down, married and launched the baby boom.

Leon mustered out of the service in January of 1946, and he immediately began looking for a job. Before long, he had one as a salesman at Tanner's Hardware and Appliance in the 700 block of Indiana.

Sam had already returned and gone to work in the advertising department of the *Times* and *Record News*, and when Nat got home in March of 1946, he, too, went back to work at the newspaper.

Leon and Sam had just been waiting on Nat's discharge to start up The Miller Brothers Band again. As preparation, Leon had already been talking to Pauline Fulcher, who had played piano with the group before they went into the service. She was manager of the record department at Tanner's. The boys wanted her to come back as part of the group.

She agreed, and her own brother Forrest Fulcher hired on as a saxophone player. Bob Steed signed on to play drums.

The group began playing again for dances in small towns around Wichita Falls and also booked regularly at the Lakeside Pavilion at Lake Wichita.

In 1947, the band was going strong, and the boys decided to get back into the drug business, but not into the retail drugstore operation that Nat had run before going into the Navy. This time, they pooled their money and bought Merchants Wholesale Drug, and they tripled sales of the company the first year they owned it. They would work sales during the day and play at night, and their wives would fill orders while they played.

Meanwhile, their music was gaining in popularity, and at one point they considered opening a club downtown with Les Fulcher, another of Pauline's brothers, and

The Early Days

Leon Gibbs at age 3.

The Gibbs boys had to haul water in a mule-drawn wagon to their house east of Wichita Falls off what is now East Scott Street. This photo was taken in the '20s.

Nat, left, and Sam Gibbs at age 7.

The three younger Gibbs brothers at about the time the twins, Sam, left, and Nat, at right, were getting out of junior high school. Leon, center, was still in elementary school.

Sam, left, and Nat in their high-school graduation gowns. They graduated from Wichita Falls High School.

The brothers in the Gibbs family in the late 1930s included, from left, C.L., Nat, Sam, Leon and Clyde.

This family photo taken May 14, 1939, includes, from left, Nat, Leon, Cleo, Juanita, Sam, Clyde Benson, Dorothy and Clyde. Seated are Edward Leon and Delma Gibbs (Leon's mother).

Nat, left, Sam and Leon in 1940.

Leon and his mother in about 1940.

Wichita Falls

in the 1920s and 1930s

Construction was taking place on every corner at Eighth and Scott Street in 1918.

Wichita Falls was a booming community in 1919. This photo was taken from Eighth and Lamar looking east. The old Kemp Hotel is at left. Behind it is the Clint Wood Building, later the First Wichita National Bank. At right is the City National Bank Building. Behind it is the National Bank of Commerce, later the Staley Building.

This 1919 photo looks west on Seventh Street from the railroad into downtown.

Oil exchanges did a landslide business in Wichita Falls during the early Burkburnett boom days. This photo, taken in May 1919, is of the Central Stock Exchange.

The oil boom days sent men into crowded streets in Wichita Falls. This 1920 photo was taken at Eighth looking north on Indiana.

Wichita County's first paved highway connected Lake Wichita with Wichita Falls. This photo shows the Lake Wichita end of the concrete strip with the exposition at the lake in the background. The photo was taken in 1919 or 1920.

The pavilion at Lake Wichita, shown here in the 1919-1920 time period, was a popular night spot for years, and the Gibbs Brothers played there early on.

In May 1920, trucks gathered on Ohio Street in Wichita Falls for a parade tour through several other North Texas communities.

About 1920, Texas Electric Service Co. installed transformers to the Wichita Motor Co., as the company kept pace with the increasing demand for lights.

Times Record News archives

Later in the 1920s, construction continued on multi-story buildings in downtown Wichita Falls. This photo looks east on Eighth Street. The building at right in the foreground is the City National Bank building with the National Bank of Commerce behind it.

The Kemp Hotel and other buildings border paved streets in this photo taken in the late '20s or early 1930s.

Besides enduring the Great Depression in the '30s, Wichita Falls residents also had to contend with the Dust Bowl. In this 1936 photo, a huge dust cloud pours over the community.

The Wichita Daily Times at its original location.

This photo of the backshop of the Wichita Falls Times was taken in the late 1930s. Leon, Nat and Sam would have been familiar with this sight.

Before the newspaper offices were moved to 1301 Lamar St., this was the chaotic view of a late night spent inserting pre-printed products into the newspaper, a job the Gibbs brothers performed in the late '30s.

Military photos

Sam Gibbs in 1944.

Nat Gibbs in 1944.

Leon Gibbs in his Army Infantry uniform before shipping out to the Philippines.

Leon Gibbs in 1944.

The Gibbs Brothers

The Miller Brothers Orchestra

The Miller Brothers Band

The earliest known photo of the Gibbs Brothers ready to play. They are, from left, Nat, Leon and Sam. This photo was taken in the 1930s.

The Miller Brothers in 1941 was comprised of, from left, Lee Cochran on trumpet, Dutch Ingram on drums, Jerry Byler on fiddle, Leon Gibbs on fiddle, Sam Gibbs on guitar, Dewayne Bass on steel guitar and Madge Suttee on piano.

Another iteration of The Miller Brothers in 1941 included, from left, Lee Cochran on trumpet, Bill Heath on saxophone, Sam Gibbs on guitar, Bob Steed on drums, Leon Gibbs on fiddle, a temporary and unidentified steel guitarist, and Madge Suttee on piano.

In the early 1940s, the band included, from left, Sam Gibbs at rear on guitar, Bill Heath at front on saxophone, Lee Cochran on trumpet in front, Bob Steed on drums behind him, Leon Gibbs, standing, Pauline Fulcher on piano and Harvey Wilson on steel guitar.

The band in this early '40s photo was comprised of, from left, Pete Martinez on steel guitar, J.E. Gose on banjo, Tom Crago, who was a KWFT announcer and not a member of the band, Nat Gibbs on bass, Sam Gibbs on guitar and Leon Gibbs on fiddle.

The band included silly skits even in the early 1940s as seen in this photo. From left are Lee Cochran on trumpet, Bob Steed, Tommy Bruce, Nat Gibbs on bass, Dewayne Bass on steel guitar and Madge Suttee on piano.

Another skit is depicted in this photo from the early 1940s. From left are Sam Gibbs on guitar, Bob Steed, Tommy Bruce and Leon Gibbs at the mike, Nat Gibbs on bass and Dewayne Bass on steel guitar.

At times the band played with guest artists. In this 1943 photo they are shown with T. Texas Tyler, at center. Band members are, from left, Nat Gibbs, Jerry Byler, Dewayne Bass, Tyler, Bill Madry, Leon Gibbs and Lee Cochran.

Another 1943 shot of the band shows it was comprised of, from left, Fats Potts, Nat Gibbs, Pete Martinez on steel guitar, J.E. Gose on banjo, Sam Gibbs on guitar, Bill Sharpe, announcer for KWFT, Lloyd Peeler on sax and Leon Gibbs on fiddle.

Bill Jourdan played steel guitar, left, and Paul Neicewanger played guitar in the band for this early 1945 photo.

Leon Gibbs at the microphone in 1946, after leaving the service.

After the war, the Miller Brothers got back together and again played with T. Texas Tyler, at the microphone. The band in this 1946 photo included, from left, Dewayne Bass on steel guitar, Jerry Byler on fiddle, Dutch Ingram on drums, Tyler, Lee Cochran on trumpet, Leon Gibbs on fiddle and a sit-in temporary guitarist.

Tommy Duncan, who had been with Bob Wills and the Texas Playboys, joined the Miller Brothers in 1946. He is in the white hat in this photo, which also shows him looking over the book he wrote about his experiences. Band members were, from left, Madge Suttee, Dewayne Bass, Dutch Ingram (behind Duncan), Sam Gibbs, Leon Gibbs, Jerry Byler and Lee Cochran.

Another 1946 photo shows these band members, from left, Lee Cochran on trumpet, Sam Gibbs on guitar, Bill Heath on sax, Bob Steed on drums, Leon Gibbs on fiddle, Pauline Fulcher on piano and Bill Jourdan on steel guitar.

The skits continued after the war. In this photo taken in 1946 or 1947, Dutch Ingram, left, carries on with Leon Gibbs, who wears a uniform with a preposterous number of service stripes on its sleeve.

Bill Jourdan and Leon Gibbs take up percussion instruments for this number, shot in 1946 or 1947.

Jim McGraw played bass with the band and Madge Suttee played piano. This photo was taken in 1947.

The band in 1947 included, from left, Bill Jourdan on steel guitar, Billy Thompson on guitar, Leon Gibbs on fiddle, Dutch Ingram on drums, Lee Cochran on trumpet, Paschalle Williams on bass, Troy Jordan on fiddle and Madge Suttee on piano.

In 1948, the M-B Trio included Jerry Byler, left, Leon Gibbs and Lee Cochran.

Billy Peeler was driver of the new stretch Chevrolet limo the Miller Brothers had built for touring. This photo was taken in 1953.

In 1954, the band was voted No. 3 in the country. Members included, from left, Bill Jourdan on steel guitar, Billy Thompson on guitar, Leon Gibbs on fiddle, Dutch Ingram on drums, Troy Jordan on fiddle, Paschalle Williams on bass, Madge Suttee on piano and Lee Cochran on trumpet.

The group in 1955 was comprised of, from left, Bill Taylor, Dutch Ingram, Bill Jourdan, Leon Gibbs, Madge Suttee, Billy Thompson, Lee Cochran and Dale Wilson.

Madge Suttee after marriage became Madge Bolin, and is shown here in 1955.

At the end of the 1950s, the band was comprised of, from left, Bill Jourdan on steel guitar, Smiley Weaver on guitar, Leon Gibbs on fiddle, Dutch Ingram on drums, Sam Gibbs on bass, Jerry Byler on fiddle, Madge Bolin on piano and Lee Cochran on trumpet. Sam Gibbs was just sitting in for this photo.

In 1959, the M-B Trio was Billy Thompson, Leon Gibbs, and Lee Cochran.

The 1959 band included, from left, Bill Jourdan on steel guitar, Billy Thompson on guitar, Leon Gibbs on fiddle, Dutch Ingram on drums, Dale Wilson on fiddle, Bill Taylor on bass, Madge Bolin on piano and Lee Cochran on trumpet.

Leon Gibbs is joined on fiddle by Bobby Rhoades in this 1961 or 1962 photo. When Leon decided to leave the band, he sold it to Rhoades.

Few if any still photos exist of the band that performed in the movie "The Last Picture Show." This photo was shot off of a television screen. Band members that can be identified are, from left, Bob Lemley on bass, Jimmy Boggs on guitar, Leon Gibbs on fiddle and Grady Solomon on guitar.

Sam Gibbs stands in front of the M-B Corral. This photo was taken in 1984.

Times Record News archives

Related Bands

Ads featuring The Miller Brothers

Leon Gibbs says that he'd vote for Hank Thompson in his Brazos Valley Boys as the No. 1 group in Western Swing in the early 1960s.

When Jimmie Davis ran for governor of Louisiana, he inevitably asked Leon Gibbs to join his band. Davis wrote "You Are My Sunshine."

Rickenbacker, the maker of quality musical instruments and related amplification gear, had a deal with the Miller Brothers for years. In return for lending the band equipment, the company got to use their likeness and name in endorsement ads such as this one.

Listen to the New Sound . . .

MILLER BROS. BAND

The Most Versatile Dance Band in the Western Field

4 Recording Artists

THE NO. 3 BAND OF THE NATION

C. & W. JAMBOREE — June 1956 . . . . . No. 3

BILLBOARD — Nov. 10, 1956 . . . . . . No. 3

CASHBOX — July 14, 1956
29 per cent
of total votes
as most promising
UP & COMING
BAND

MANAGEMENT
SAM GIBBS
1540 HANOVER
WICHITA FALLS, TEXAS

Latest Releases

• "Long Gone Caro"
• "Way Must It Be"
• "Hey Pretty Baby"
• "As You Were Stand-ing By My Side"
• "Happy Birthday Dear Jesus"

M-B TRIO
Voted No. 9 Vocal
Group in Dec 1956
C & W JAMBOREE

DANCE

LEON Miller
and the
MILLER Bros.

4-Star Recording Artist
PLUS
M-B TRIO

Dance

A *New* SOUND in
WESTERN SWING

LEON MILLER
and the No. 3 Band
of the Nation

Miller Bros.

FEATURING

M-B TRIO
4-Star Recording Artist

Last Flings

(Spring 2001 & Spring 2002)

Members of the Over the Hill Band backed up Leon Gibbs for his first Last Fling, a dance held to celebrate his 80th birthday.

12 31 '01

Leon Gibbs plays with the Over the Hill Band in the 2001 Last Fling.

Leon received recognition for his more than 70 years in music. Ken Schnick and Mary Lou Steed made the presentation.

Leon shows off the recognition plaque presented to him for 70 years in music.

The Second Last Fling

Leon Gibbs of the Miller Bros. Band

Leon "Miller" Gibbs

10.00 each

BYOB
Set-ups Available

Wally   *Jimmy*   *Frank*   *Mickey*   *Hank*
Hendrixson   *Via*   *Farnsworth*   *Stoddard*   *Whitson*

Saturday April 27, 2002 7:00-11:00 pm
Knights of Columbus Hall
on Turtle Creek Road
Tickets Available @ Sam Gibbs Music
and BJD Engraving

Gary Lawson

Before the band started playing for the second Last Fling in 2002, Leon got a big hug from his great-granddaughter, Teddi Schmidt, left, and his great-granddaughter, Taylor Lay.

Gary Lawson

Granddaughter Christi Schmidt greets Leon during the second Last Fling.

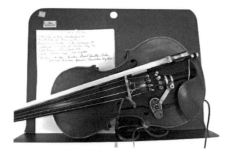

Leon's fiddle stand has notes about people he wants to introduce during the second Last Fling.

Leon concentrates on his music.

All by Gary Lawson

Leon plays to get warmed up for the second Last Fling.

Students

At the second Last Fling, Leon visited with two students, Kyle Aaron Lopez, left, and the author.

Brooke Whyrick started learning fiddle from Leon when she was just 3 years old.

Ryan Hager is the little cowboy reading the music. Leon is on the fiddle playing the Petrolia Jamboree.

Ryan Phillips took fiddle from Leon.

Chad Odom took guitar lessons from Leon. This photo was taken in August 1992.

Kyle Aaron Lopez, another of Leon's students, plays fiddle with Leon at the first Last Fling in 2001. He returned to play again at the second Last Fling in 2002.

Members
of the Family

Leon and Sam appeared at the Legends of Western Swing festival in Wichita Falls in 2001 to accept membership in the Legends of Western Swing Hall of Fame.

Sam Gibbs met with Texas Gov. Preston Smith when the governor declared Bob Wills Week in Texas.

Nat Gibbs,
taken in
about 2000.

Gary Lawson

Leon Gibbs in 2002 was still teaching guitar and fiddle at Sam Gibbs Music Co. on Jacksboro Highway, owned by Paula and Steve Moore. Paula is the daughter of Sam Gibbs.

In the late 1980s, the Gibbs siblings got together for this photo. They are, from left, Leon, Juanita, Sam and Nat.

Leon and his wife, Audrey, celebrate his 80th birthday in 2001 at a dance in Archer City.

Gary Lawson

Leon Gibbs in 2002.

CHAPTER 9

There'd never been a "Miller" in the Miller Brothers, and by 1950, there weren't any brothers in there, either.

Even without his brothers, Leon continued to run the Miller Brothers Club on Travis Street and to pull together good musicians, some to play in the band as people rotated in and out of this fairly itinerant and impermanent business and some to play at the club.

Leon remembered, for example, Billy Walker who worked for KWFT Radio in Wichita Falls and also sang with the Miller Brothers before going out on his own with Sam as his booking agent.

"He was real good and later on – he stayed here about a year – he moved to Nashville and he joined the Grand Ole Opry, and he stayed there till his death. He recorded on Continental Records, and he did well in Nashville," Leon said.

Another standout player who stuck with the Miller Brothers for years was Madge Suttee, who played piano and recorded with Lefty Frizzell on six of his early recordings, including "Mom and Dad's Waltz," "You Got the Money, Honey, I Got the Time," and a song called "Always Late," one that was directly due to a deal Frizzell made with Leon. It seems The Miller Brothers had an old Greyhound bus they used to travel from town to town, and Frizzell bought the bus from Leon knowing full well that it had been ridden hard. Leon said Frizzell told him he wrote "Always Late" because of that bus.

In 1952, Leon began talking about moving to a more permanent and bigger place, and Lee Cochran struck up a conversation on the matter with Gene and Clellie Wagner, who were regular customers at the Travis location.

"Gene had been doing real well in oil," Leon says, "but he was getting weary of it or something, or wanted to expand, so he wanted us to go in partners and build a club."

In addition to Leon and his wife, the group formed to run the operation included Lee and Ellie Cochran, Gene and Clellie Wagner, and Sam and Marvel Gibbs.

The partners bought 10 acres on Sheppard Access Road in the north part of Wichita Falls and had it cleared and a new building constructed there of prefab steel and sheet metal.

They called it the M-B Corral, and when it opened, Sam and Gene had already booked some top names besides the Miller Brothers, who played regularly on Wednesdays and Fridays and Saturdays. And not all of them were country. Tommy Dorsey and Harry James were scheduled to bring their orchestras to town. But so were Bob Wills and Lefty Frizzell.

From the outset, the M-B Corral was better than a run-of-the-mill dance hall or club. For one thing, it was brand new. For another, it served no alcoholic beverages. "Just Cokes, 7-Up, a bucket of ice," Leon said. "Hey, there's more money in ice than there was anything out there." Actually, in that, he was just kidding because the partners were smart enough to count the empties when the night was over, empties that people had brought in themselves. "Lord, they'd bring in their ice keg full of beer and set it under the table," Leon said. "That was permissible. But we didn't sell it."

Over time, however, the partners figured out they were not maximizing their potential in terms of beverage sales. "Cleaning up those bottles, you realize how much drinking was going on," he said. "So we bought a building, remodeled it, put it out on the highway and opened up a package store. Man, this thing moved."

But "in one year's time we were robbed twice."

The manager of the place got so disgusted, he quit, selling his share to the other partners. They stayed in business, however, only about 12 months before closing it down.

Business, meanwhile, was booming at the M-B Corral, thanks in part to a cooperative effort between the owners and KWFT Radio. The Miller Brothers had a 12:30 p.m. radio show every day that was taped at the M-B Corral. The radio station also broadcast live from the Corral on Saturday nights.

This arrangement helped the club attract visiting bands, because those bands were able to fill the one-hour time slot on Saturdays and also record the taped program for the noon hour. In those broadcasts, they were allowed to hype their next appearance locations and times.

When the club first opened, it had a stated and posted capacity of 700 people, but Leon said between 900 and 1,000 was the typical crowd. No more than a few months had passed before the foundation was poured to expand the club to actually accommodate the number attending. The men paid $1.25 apiece for an evening of dancing. The women paid $1.

Shortly after the M-B Corral opened, the first band booked from outside was Bob Wills and the Texas Playboys. For awhile, he set the record for largest crowd drawn to the club, but that record was broken permanently several months later by The Miller Brothers Band itself.

The members of the band earned a weekly salary, getting paid once a week, every Saturday night after the crowd had left.

With Nat and Sam both gone and with the new club,

the Miller Brothers Band got some new personnel. Leon continued to play lead fiddle and was the band's leader. He hired Johnny Lytel from Fort Worth as his harmony fiddle player. Paschalle Williams played bass, Lee Cochran was on trumpet, Dutch Ingram was on drums, Madge Suttee on piano, Billy Thompson on guitar and Bill Jourdan on steel guitar.

Over the years the M-B became the best venue to showcase musical talent in the North Texas-Southern Oklahoma area.

"It was the biggest and most popular honky tonk in Wichita Falls," Gary Gregg, who played guitar with The Mammals, a Wichita Falls-based rock band in the 1960s, told a *Times* reporter in 1984. "There was nothing like it except in Dallas. M-B showcased all the early rock 'n' roll, then country-western music.

"It was a club that the Rolling Stones would love to play in today. You could really get into the music you were playing, and the close-quartered crowd just loved it."

Big-name entertainers all eventually found their way to the M-B from opening night to closing time.

With the M-B Corral, the Gibbs brothers and other investors were riding a tidal wave that had started after the end of World War II and the literal demise of most of the big bands that had dominated the music scene before the war, a tidal wave that would eventually lead also to the demise of The Miller Brothers Band itself.

But in the 50s, when the M-B Corral was just getting started, it was the season for singers (*All The Years* 459). Thanks to the popularity of singles records, the rise in influence of disc jockeys and their shows, and the emergence of a star system that later made its way into every family's living room, thanks to television's pervasive growth, demand was huge for the kinds of music that Sam could book and the M-B Corral could feature other than, of course, country music and Western swing, its staples.

Realizing that rock 'n' roll was here to stay (something Leon said he neglected to pick up on – he said he told members of his band that rock had a lifetime of no more than six months.), Sam let it roll right through the corral and other places in this area.

Rock had its critics, of course, and its analyzers, people whose job it was to figure out why young people caught one wave of pop culture and not another. One such critic had this to say about the music that swept through in the 50s:

> Rock 'n' roll was a narcotic, an intoxicant, an hallucinogenic. It created a catatonic state not only among the listeners but even among the performers themselves. It was music of protest. The young related to it because they were in ferment, protesting not so much against the evils of society (that would come in the 1960s) as against the moral and ethical standards of the establishment. Of the momentous events that swept the fifties to change the face of American society, the young seemed hardly conscious. ... The interests of the young lay in their own insulated world. ..." (*All The Years* 556)

That was also true of the stars who seemed to come out of nowhere, like a young man from Memphis, Tennessee, who changed the face of rock 'n' roll early on. Before he had a big name and millions of fans, Elvis Presley made it to the M-B Corral, and Sam told a reporter about his appearance in the 1984 *Wichita Falls Times* piece, recalling that Elvis was just a shy kid who made a $3.65 long-distance call to his mother from the nightclub.

Elvis was paid $125 for his night's work at the Corral. Within two months, Sam said, he "was asking $50,000 and getting it."

About that same time, Fats Domino made an appearance at the M-B Corral, and he was asking for $400.

"We wanted (instead) to give him 70 percent of the gate," Sam said. "We lost money on him." They gave him the $400.

Others who played the M-B over the years included Jerry Lee Lewis, whose piano-playing style Leon likened to that of Madge Suttee, The Miller Brothers' longtime pianist, along with Ike and Tina Turner, Little Richard, B.B. King, Lionel Hampton, Bo Diddley, Chuck Berry, Roger Miller, Conway Twitty, and Ray Price (*Times*, July 15, 1984: 1F).

While Leon was working with the band to make sure it was in top form for the regular club performances, he was also working to get things ready for steady touring around the country. He wanted to extend the band's reach beyond just the small circle of towns around Wichita Falls.

In preparation for that, he had a special bus built for the band by the Ambruster & Co. of Fort Smith, Arkansas. Using a standard 1953 Chevrolet, the company cut it in half and extended it so that it was a Chevy limousine big enough to carry all the group. In addition, Leon had special uniforms made up for the members of the band so they sported similar outfits. And each member had several outfits that they would rotate in and out of for different shows.

Sometimes, however, they ran into odd customs when it came to what was acceptable to wear on a gig.

For example, they learned not to wear their cowboy hats while playing onstage at certain Air Force bases because if you wore a hat it meant you were buying the drinks, Leon discovered. But most of the time people recognized the outfits for what they were – part of the show.

One time, though, a drunk airman tried to pick a

fight with Leon over the group's outfits in a base club.

"Hey, cowboy, where's your horse?" the young man said.

"So, I went over there," Leon said. "I thought, well, I'd get him to quit hollering *Hey, cowboy!* So, I went past his table, and I said, 'I hope you guys are having a lot of fun. Is there any song we can play for you?' And that same little guy said, 'No, where's your horse?' I said, 'I left him outside.' He said, 'Well, I thought you might ride him in here.' Still needling me. I didn't want to cause any trouble. He said, 'Well, where IS your horse?' I said, 'He's outside, but,' I said, 'I am talking to his ass right now.'

"He looked at me. I looked down and saw this kid's foot sticking out. I don't know why I did this, but I raised my foot up and I stomped that kid with my boots on. I stomped that kid's foot, he let out a yell, and I said, 'Son, you'd better watch it. Some of these cowboys around here might just stomp the hell out of you.' I batted him on the shoulder and walked off."

As part of the regular show, the members of the group also put together something unusual for country and western bands of the time. Taking a page from vaudeville and the Grand Ol' Opry and foreshadowing what would be called "variety shows" on television, the Miller Brothers did their own floor show.

An evening of entertainment with the Miller Brothers, then, would include two sets of straight dancing or listening music along with a brief set of skits. In one set, Leon was featured wearing an Army uniform with service stripes reaching past his fingertips but with only a private's rank on his sleeves. Any service member or veteran would know this was a fellow who'd been nothing but trouble.

That particular segment was scripted around a song that involved a woman who had written a "Dear

John" letter to her boyfriend overseas.

The skits were mainly jokes, some of them one-liners, many of them off-color.

Some examples:

• There was a man who had his throat operated on, but he insisted that he couldn't make it through the day without his coffee. So the nurses decided to give him his coffee rectally. When they did so, he flinched. "Was it too hot?" they asked.

"Nope," he said. "Too sweet."

• Did you hear about the Aggies who were driving down the road and saw a sign that said, "Clean Restrooms Ahead."

They cleaned six before they got to where they were going.

• Then there was this single woman who was the subject of much speculation among the church ladies, who considered her to be wild and loose.

One Sunday after church, she stopped to shake hands with the preacher, who was standing at the doorway, and he said, "I prayed for you last night."

"Well," she said, "then why didn't you call? I could have been here in 10 minutes."

• How about the kid who is practicing his violin lessons, and the dog is standing at his door howling.

The kid's dad hollers at the kid: "Can't you play something the dog doesn't know?"

They were corny, but they got laughs, and the crowds seemed to enjoy the skit portion of The Miller Brothers shows, Leon said. In fact, when the floor show portion of the evening began, people would leave their seats and come stand around the bandstand.

About the same time the band was doing skits, it was also figuring out other ways to vary a night of entertainment. Leon was joined by Billy Thompson on guitar and Lee Cochran to form what was first called the Panhandle Trio and later on The Miller Brothers Trio.

So at this point a typical gig would include dance music from The Miller Brothers, a set of skits from the members of the group, and separate interludes by the trio.

To complete the transition from a family group to something bigger and more mobile, the band changed its name to Leon Miller and The Miller Brothers, emphasizing the name of the leader in much the same way The Texas Playboys emphasized their star player by pulling Bob Wills' name out and putting it in front on the marquee.

Leon was proud of the "look" and the sound of his band, and was particularly thankful for the sponsorship of Rickenbacker. At the time Rickenbacker was one of the big names in the production of musical instruments and related equipment.

Rickenbacker provided all the band members' instruments, including the steel guitar, and all the amplification gear, as well.

"And once a year they would meet us, they'd know when we were going to be in California, and replace these with new amps, new guitars, new bass," Leon said. The company did not make a violin, so Leon provided his own, but he did use the Rickenbacker mandolins during his show.

Of course, when Rickenbacker put out a catalog, it would have photos of The Miller Brothers band outfitted with nothing but its own equipment.

With a new limo, new suits, new name and some new acts to spice up a show, the Miller Brothers were ready to get on the road.

Meanwhile, in its first year the M-B Corral drew big crowds who came to hear the likes of Bob Wills, Joe Carson, Ann Jones and Kenny Brewer.

But one of the biggest draws of the year was Fats Domino. Rock 'n' roll was no longer a regional phenomenon in some big cities or in Southern capitals. It was gaining a hugely broad audience, even in the Southwest, which had typically been more accepting of country and Western Swing than any other genre.

Sam Gibbs recognized this trend before just about anyone else, because he was booking bands across the country in the early 50s with his Sam Gibbs Orchestra Service and knew what the owners of roadhouses and auditoriums were wanting him to find to bring in the crowds.

At the local level, rock groups began forming, and Jack Arnold and the Flames booked through Sam, as did Tommy Strange and the Strangers, a group that played a little rock and a little pop. Vern Hickey's group was just rock 'n' roll.

So Leon, Sam and Gene decided to keep the M-B Corral open Thursday, Friday and Saturday nights. The Miller Brothers were typically booked on Thursdays and Saturdays, but Fridays were reserved for rock 'n' roll.

CHAPTER 10

The first real tour booked by Sam for Leon and The Miller Brothers was into New Mexico, and they made stops at Albuquerque, Hobbs, Clovis, Silver City, Socorro, Farmington, and Gallup.

They were gone a full week, the first in many dozens of such trips that would take them into virtually every state of the union over the next half-dozen years.

With touring now a part of their repertoire, it made sense for the group to get more involved in recording. Having recordings out and available for sale, in addition to having a regular show on local radio, would lead to an increase in interest among fans. They would want to see live and in person what they could only imagine when listening to records or radio. Likewise, if you played songs people liked when they saw you in actual performance, they might go buy them at the record store.

So Sam made a trip to Los Angeles to visit with executives at Four Star Records. He had already sent them tapes from some of the group's radio shows. The executives offered him a deal, he took it and then he booked The Miller Brothers for a cross-country tour through New Mexico and Arizona and right into Los Angeles for the taping sessions.

"We set up at 7 p.m. and recorded the song over and over until they decided that was a take," Leon said. The group did "Shanty Town" and "Under the Double Eagle," two of the songs The Miller Brothers had recorded much earlier on the Delta label.

"This time it sold real big," Leon said. "It sold big in Canada, too."

Along with "Shanty Town" and "Under the Double Eagle," the band recorded "Rose of Tijuana" and "Geronimo."

Having these records on the market and being played by radio stations all over the U.S. made the group popular quick. Nevertheless, with the occasional exception, the band was still staying close to home to play two nights a week at the M-B Corral and to play on Mondays and Tuesdays in places such as Scotland, Windthorst, Archer City, Megargel and Rhineland near Wichita Falls.

In 1954, with a successful record under their belts and with more and more requests rolling into Sam's agency to book the Miller Brothers out of town, the band was doing well. They spent much of the summer on a tour through the western part of the country. That same year, disc jockeys from throughout the country participating in a poll conducted by *Cash Box* magazine named The Miller Brothers as the No. 3 Western band in the nation.

"Man, that was a big boost for us," Leon said. "Naturally, our price went up and it was a common thing for us to get 60 percent of the door." Also in 1954, disc jockeys polled by *Cowboy Songs Magazine* ranked the band as No. 3 in the country. But it was also in 1954 that the band suffered a big, though temporary, setback.

In mid-July, the band had just finished a gig in Colorado Springs, and it was way after midnight before the limo started taking the group to the next town for the next show.

"We were traveling along and a highway patrolman came up behind us with lights flashing," Leon said. The cop had been looking for him and asked him to step out of the car and then said, "I have been told to stop you and tell you that your M-B Corral has been bombed, and it's burning at this time."

At the next town, Leon found out from Sam that

someone had broken into the club through a window, set up a bomb and the explosion had caught the club on fire.

The band finished its short tour and then headed home to help repair the club. Chairs were repaired in the garage of Leon's new house on Ninth Street, and the club was cleaned up and repainted.

On Aug. 7, it reopened.

"Whoever did this was never caught," Leon said. "We couldn't figure out anyone that would do this to us."

After the fire, though, the club was busier than ever and also just as filled with rock 'n' roll fans as country-western fans. Along with Bob Wills, Sam booked into the club B.B. King and Bo Diddley, Johnny Rodriguez and Elvis Presley.

The fire did not dent the popularity of the club or the band, which kept a hard schedule on the road and in town.

Soon, however, they discovered that they were going to have to do something they'd not had to worry about in Wichita Falls – they were going to have join the musicians union.

The local in Wichita Falls was small and was comprised of jazz and pop musicians, according to Leon's sister, Juanita, who was secretary of the union for years. Country musicians just didn't join up.

And bands like The Miller Brothers felt they didn't need to join because the outfit was already paying far more than union scale wages anyway.

"We paid what Bob Wills paid and we paid what Hank Thompson paid," Leon said. "And they knew they had a good job. And they'd stay with it until it near killed them, and then they took off."

Nevertheless, at an increasing number of clubs and concert establishments booking the band, the rules required union membership, especially when the band started playing in Las Vegas, Nevada.

"In Las Vegas, at the Golden Nugget, you are 40 minutes on and 20 minutes off," Leon said. "And when the 40 minutes is over, you'd better be winding it down, because the curtain starts to close. And when the 20 minutes is up, you'd better be standing there, because ready or not the curtains opened. That was a union deal."

Leon said he didn't mind doing business with the union. After all, it provided a good job for his baby sister. But sometimes he got irritated by some of the union representatives who tried to enforce the rules in arbitrary ways.

He recalled a run-in with a Mr. Causseana in El Paso when the man, who was head of the union, came around to a dance hall where The Miller Brothers were playing to collect the union fees on the spot.

"We were running late, and I said, 'Mr. Causseana, let us pay your fee through the office, we pay all our union stuff through the office.' 'No,' he says. 'I always collect from bands; it's better for me that way.' I said, 'Doggone, man, I'll pay you through the office.' He said, 'I want my money now.'

"So I looked at my watch and said, 'Mr. Causseana, I've got two minutes before I'm supposed to head down – I'm union, I know how to do my job. You had better do yours and get off this stand and let me work or I'm going to report you to the international. You won't let me be a good union member, and I want to quit.'

"He stepped off the stage and I told Lee Cochran, 'Pay that SOB and get rid of him.'"

One of the best things that happened to The Miller Brothers that year was attracting the interest of Tommy Duncan, who had played for Bob Wills.

Duncan had joined The Light Crust Doughboys, run by Wills, in 1932, and to understand how good he was, you have to understand how picky Wills was about who would be singing with his group. Charles Townsend, Wills' biographer, wrote that, "A vocalist for Wills had to be able to sing everything from blues to the latest popular songs, plus the traditional jazz, novelty, and cowboy songs. Finally, on Sept. 21, after Bob had auditioned 67 singers, he found his man, a young fellow from Whitney named Thomas Elmer Duncan" (*San Antonio Rose* 74).

Duncan stayed with Wills for about 15 years. "Tommy's style had that 'ripple of happiness that fit the band,' Wills once said (*San Antonio Rose* 256). But he left Wills and the Texas Playboys in 1948 after making a remark about Wills's drinking problem that Wills overheard himself.

Townsend in his biography of Wills tells about what happened:

> Duncan had been with Wills long enough to have become a famous figure in western music. He had a following of thousands of fans, and he wanted to cash in on his own popularity by forming his own band. Unfortunately for Wills, other key musicians left the band shortly after Duncan was fired. Duncan left and formed his own group called the Western All Stars. But it only lasted a couple of years. (*San Antonio Rose* 255-256)

Duncan toured with The Miller Brothers the last two months of 1953 and all of 1954, according to Leon, who said, "Tommy Duncan was one of the best things that happened to the Miller Brothers so far. When he got mail at the radio station, I would get him to dedicate a song to (whoever wrote the letter), and nine times out of 10 it was a Bob Wills song."

On the Intro label, the band backed up Duncan on songs such as "Stars Over San Antonio," "I Reckon I'm a Texan," "I Guess You Were Right," "Tennessee Church

Bells," "Hound Dog" and "That Certain Feeling."

On tour, Tommy sold a softback, magazine-style book he'd written while he also sang with the band. The book was his own biography, including details of his career with Wills and other bands. Much of it was in the form of photos.

"With the help of Tommy Duncan, we picked up a lot of clubs," Leon said, but Tommy stuck around only through the end of '54. Six or so years later, he was back on a kind of reunion tour with Bob Wills.

Touring took on a life of its own for the band in '54. In addition to playing clubs, the band was playing rodeos and other special events, such as a fund-raiser for the Ringgold Cemetery Association that featured Jimmie Davis, the Louisiana governor who wrote "You Are My Sunshine."

But in 1955, things got much more hectic and interesting.

That was, for one thing, the year that Bob Wills and his Texas Playboys became affiliated with the Sam Gibbs Orchestra Service. This gave additional credibility to an agency that was already booking some of the biggest regional stars.

Through the club and on the road, the Miller Brothers found themselves playing with big-name personalities such as Buck Owens, Webb Pierce, Tex Williams, Tex Ritter, Hank Williams, and Brenda Lee.

For the most part, the stars were easy to get along with, as Leon remembered them. He recalled one run-in, however, with Webb Pierce when the tour was in Washington state at a skating rink filled mostly with kids.

Leon remembered introducing Pierce, who came onstage with a fifth of whiskey in his hand. He set the whisky down on the top of the piano.

And a guy ran up there and said, 'I can't start

this until he moves that bottle,' and he said, 'Webb, move your bottle or you'll get me in trouble.' [Webb says] 'no, no, I'm not going to take a drink for awhile.' So, he turned around, told me the song he was going to sing – I forget what it was – and I said, 'Webb, the man told me not to start the song.' So, he said, 'No, 'I'm not moving the bottle. Kick if off, boys' – whatever song it was. I said, 'Webb, we are going to take an intermission. What are you going to do?' He said, 'I guess I'm going to move this damn bottle.' And he did.

Later on in Fort Worth, Webb Pierce pulled the same stunt, Leon said, and ultimately took refuge with his bottle in the women's restroom – "and they had to send a lady in there to get him."

The prospect that his band members were drinking on the job did consume some of Leon's time while The Miller Brothers were on tour.

About the same time of the Webb Pierce incident, the band was booked to back up T. Texas Tyler on a small tour he'd put together.

"He would sometimes drink a little too much," Leon remembered. "In Truth or Consequences, New Mexico, he had just bought a new white hat. (Someone had got off with his old one.) I introduced him, and a girl right by the stage grabbed his hat. She kissed it and left her lip prints and gave it back to him. He looked at it and threw it out into the crowd.

"In Cheyenne, Wyoming, I introduced him and he came up on the band stand and started preaching. He had been really preaching for about five minutes, and the people were really listening. I motioned for the band to follow me. We got off the band stand, and a few minutes later he stopped preaching and looked around and said, 'Where's my damn band?' We went right back."

In the main, though, neither the members of the band nor the musicians they played with had much to do with drinking, other than, of course, Bob Wills, who was famous for not holding his liquor.

Leon said he had rules that "you just didn't drink when you were working," rules, incidentally, that he broke later on during a period that could only be characterized as burn-out.

Along with the no-drinking rule went the warning from Leon that anyone caught drinking on the job would be dropped from the tour right where they were at the time, and the delinquent could just find his own way home.

Only once, Leon said, did he remember having trouble enforcing that rule.

That was when the band went to Puerto Rico for a series of performances, and one member got drunk during show-time.

"The job was over so I went up to his room, ordered some coffee, sobered him up, and I said, 'Man, I can't fire you here but I will look for the opportunity when it comes, so you decide," Leon said. "He never drank on us again. He never drank on us again" (Chance interview, 1999).

The band also had rules about women, and Leon rarely mentioned any situations involving women other than his children and wives.

For one thing, when the band was on the road it was, literally, on the road, going from town to town for a long series of one-night concerts, so there was no real way to stay hooked up to a woman for very long, even for one night.

Occasionally, the group had longer gigs. Leon recalled that every summer for seven or eight years the band played for the big rodeo in Cheyenne, Wyoming. Since they were going to be in one place for a period of time, the members of the band rented a couple of three-bedroom apartments in a motel that came equipped with a kitchen. Lee Cochran would cook.

"We had a rule about bringing women in this place," Leon said. "You couldn't do it, see – unless she slept with everybody." He paused and grinned. "You could not bring your women in this room."

Touring became almost routine during the 50s for the band, and early on the Miller Brothers saw a lot of personnel turnover (Chance interview, 1999).

One year, Chance was told, they were on the road more than 300 days. And "on the road" was where they spent most of their time, because of the distances involved.

One reporter did some figuring on the subject, counting mileage driven for the year 1956 alone. Here's what he counted up (Tricker, et al):

June 10: Ogden, Utah; June 11: Ontario, Oregon, a distance of 350 miles; June 12, Lewiston, Idaho, a distance of 180 miles; June 13: Mountain Home, Idaho, a distance of 280 miles; June 14: Potlach, Idaho, a distance of 300 miles; June 15, Moses Lake, Washington, a distance of 120 miles; June 16 and 17, Spokane, Washington, a distance of 120 miles; June 18 and 19: Mountain Home, Idaho, a distance of 400 miles; June 20: Twin Falls, Idaho, a distance of 80 miles; June 21: Grand Junction, Colorado, a distance of 250 miles; June 22: Albuquerque, New Mexico, a distance of 320 miles; June 23: Farmington, New Mexico, a distance of 150 miles; June 24 and 25, rest days; June 26: Alamosa, Colorado, a distance of 250 miles; June 27: Pueblo, Colorado, a distance of 150 miles; June 28: Lander, Wyoming, a distance of 340 miles; June 29: Cheyenne, Wyoming, a distance of 225 miles; and June

30: Grand Junction, Colo., a distance of 250 miles.
That's nearly 4,000 miles in 21 days.

The constant summertime touring – a bus could easily rack up 100,000 miles a year with the Miller Brothers Band — took its toll on family life, of course, but the band members did their best to get together with their wives and children when they could. In fact, sometimes Leon and the other married members took advantage of a bus breakdown to have their wives come see them. That happened with a bus breakdown in Alamogordo, New Mexico, when he and Lee Cochran called their wives to drive over from Wichita Falls.

"So they brought us a car, and like all other breakdowns, we got them motel rooms there in Alamogordo, and the bus driver stayed there, and they were there for four days ...," Leon said. Meanwhile, the band members took the cars and headed out to play their gigs. Then, when the bus was repaired, the wives and children joined the band on the bus.

Another time the band came in from a concert tour in Bermuda and Leon's and Lee's wives were there to meet them and go on to Chicago.

Leon's daughters have their own memories of those rare times when they were able to meet up with the bus and the band.

Daughter Carole said she remembered seeing drunk cowboys passed out in the streets of Cheyenne, Wyoming, and swiping oranges off trees beside the highway in California and eating dinner prepared over a campfire by Indians in Canada.

"We were in Minot, North Dakota, walking downtown one day," she recalled. "All of a sudden money came floating down in the air. We looked up and saw money blowing out of an open window in a bank building. Everyone started running about, trying to catch as much money as they could. We didn't get hardly any because all the adults beat us to it."

Daughter Patsy said she remembered catching blue crabs in the ocean from a pier at Fort Walton Beach, Florida, using chicken necks as bait, and eating crabs after her mom cooked them right there.

Another tour-related memory was a scary ocean encounter.

"Daddy and I were swimming in the ocean and a baby hammerhead shark was swimming all around us," she said. "A man caught the shark off of a pier. We were trying to run in waist-deep water to get out and everyone was scared to death we would be attacked by the shark."

But, for the most part, touring was just a hectic business, going from one town to the next, trying to remember where you were when you got on stage.

Over the years, Leon lost a number of good players but also replaced them without, in his own mind, ever diminishing the quality of the music. Touring was tough, especially for men and women with families, and eventually it took its toll on Leon, too.

"I remember," Carole wrote in a letter to her dad, "you traveling hundreds of miles home so you could attend my high-school graduation. You only got to stay home about 48 hours and had to turn around and go back. I never really thanked you properly for that. I didn't realize, I guess, how hard and tiring that must have been for you. Anyway, I've never forgotten it, and thank you."

Looking back, Leon sometimes seems incredulous at the pace the band kept and the good spirits that prevailed:

I tell you, on the road – I don't know how we did what we did. And it just kind of makes you grouchy – and this may sound funny – not drinking, not smoking (we never had but one guy picked two marijuana sticks down in Del Rio across the border, and he got fired over that. We did not allow that.) But, when you get up and say, 'We are glad to see you tonight in Dallas,' and, Lord, Dallas was last night, and somebody would holler out a different name, Fort Worth, El Paso, Houston. But Madge always knew where we were. And it has happened, you don't even know where you are. And after you had been out there as long as we were, you don't care where you are.

Tough as it was, however, and while some of the events tend to blend together or blur over time, going on tour made for a lot of memorable experiences for Leon, who looked back now mainly at the adventure and fun of it all.

He talked fondly of the band's tours with Jimmie Davis, who had been governor of Louisiana, and used, as did some Texas gubernatorial candidates, a country band to create excitement and draw a crowd. Davis had written "You Are My Sunshine," a tune he played at every stop.

"The first time we played for Jimmie Davis, Sam quoted him a price, and he said, 'That's fine,'" Leon said. "And when we got through he said the check will be in the mail – I said, 'No problem, Jimmie.' And the check was for more than we asked for. On all the deals there was never a price quoted to Jimmie Davis again, because he'd always pay more than you asked him. We just left it up to him, and the check came from [a company that backed Davis called Billups Oil Co.]."

One summer the band was on a train with Davis when he left Louisiana to go to the Astrodome in Houston to sing the National Anthem at the start of a game:

He told me before we went up there, 'For goodness sake, Leon, hum the key we are playing in.' So, I said, 'OK,' so we hit him a chord, and the organ player up there had just been playing some stuff before us, and we were pretty much in tune with the organ player. But nothing was arranged. We hit Jimmie a chord, and he walked right by me and said, 'Oooooh say can you see ...' and, boy, he got up there and the people after he got through – well he made a hit, but he was the most humble, the nicest man you'll ever meet.

One summer, the Miller Brothers were booked by Jimmie Davis to join him on a train tour sponsored by the Shreveport Chamber of Commerce.

"We were on this train three nights and four days," Leon said. "Everybody wore a big plantation hat, and in practically every town of any size this train would stop and they would make speeches – we would unload the instruments, get out there ready to play – you talk about a job, this was a job."

In mid-1956, Four Star Records announced that one week would be Miller Brothers Week in Texas, and they advertised throughout the state and announced it on radio stations in the major cities. Free records of the band's songs were sent to disc jockeys as part of the promotion.

The week started at the M-B Corral in Wichita Falls on Saturday night, and then the band was off to Odessa for Sunday night, then to El Paso, Del Rio, Corpus Christi, Fort Worth, Dallas, and back home.

"I wish I could remember the miles – my friend, when you leave El Paso, it's a long way," Leon said. "It sold a lot of records, though."

At another point, the band was in the Ozarks and wound up on the Red Foley show taped for television. The show was taped on a Saturday night, and featured, along with The Miller Brothers, Brenda Lee, a pop singer. The taped show was to be played the following Saturday night, and the band was to be back at the M-B Corral for that evening. Sam rented TV sets for the event and set them up all around the club so that people could watch The Miller Brothers on television while also seeing them in person.

As their fame increased, the touring became more intense and the band began taking to the road during the winter months as well as the summer months.

One winter, the bus was heading home on U.S. 66 and ran into a snowstorm at the Texas-New Mexico line. Finally, traffic came to a dead stop when a truck ahead of them jack-knifed under a railroad trestle.

"We'd just taken on 40 gallons of gas on either side [of the bus]," Leon said. "We had a 40-gallon tank on one side, and a 40-gallon tank on the other side, so we had 80 gallons of gas. Traffic was stopped. I don't know how many cars were ahead of us, and I don't know how many were behind us. But, boy, people began running out of gas, and we went up and down the cars there, and people with kids – or anybody who wanted to, we invited back to the bus. And we opened our bunk beds up and they could put their kids up there, and we had covers for them. And this bus had a front heater and a back heater, just like air conditioners. And, man, this was around 5 o'clock in the afternoon, because we were supposed to be home by 9 to play the M-B Corral, and this little train came out and picked up a load and took them back to this little town."

The band members were among those who made the short trek, leaving the bus on the highway, and they wound up staying two days in a small school house with other stranded travelers.

As the roads began to reopen, the band members hired a truck to retrieve their instruments from the bus and they set up and played a full show for those still unable to leave the school house.

These tours almost always took The Miller Brothers to military installations, and many of their gigs were for service members.

"We played practically every Army and Navy base in Texas," Leon said.

When the band had a gig at a military club, Leon would find out the name of the commanding officer, and if the commander happened to be in the club that night, Leon would also find out the officer's favorite song – "and I found out real quick, if he dances the first dance you are in for a good night. Because they'd all hit the floor because he did. It's unbelievable how that was. And if he didn't dance, man, you'd struggle and finally get 'em going if you were lucky."

One time, the band was booked to play at Fort Bliss in El Paso, Texas, but Sam got an urgent call from the NCO club at Yuma, Arizona, pressuring him to send the band there instead.

"They said they really needed us because they were having pilots from all over for a big get-together," Leon said. "They said be at the (Sheppard) Air Force runway at 9 a.m., and a plane would pick us up. Our bus driver had us out there, and we unloaded our equipment and they loaded us on the plane and flew us to Yuma, Arizona."

Frankie McWhorter, a good fiddle player who was also a rancher, joined the band right before it was leaving on a tour. Leon said:

We were going overseas – Canada. But from there we flew into Greenland. Frankie said, 'I can't take a shot' (if you hadn't had them, you had to take a shot before the Air Force took you places). I mean, he was riding these broke horses, breaking these horses and the head of this ranch – well, you know those guys are tough – and he said, "I promise you I'll faint," and I said, "I'll be right behind you and I'll catch you." Well, this doctor pulls out this needle, we all had our shirts off. He starts at Frankie, and Frankie fell down. So, this doctor looked at me, and he says, "We might as well shoot him; he's got to have it." I said, go ahead, and he was out. And he got his shot and they gave him some water, and he came to, and he was all right after that.

By 1958, after nearly a decade of ever-increasing tour dates, the band began to lose key personnel.

Madge Suttee, the stalwart pianist for the band since its raw beginnings after the war, fell in love with the military manager of an Air Force Club, Bruce Bolin, and she and Bruce were married that year and she left the band, replaced by Curly Hollingsworth, who also drove the bus and fixed it when it broke down. "He earned his money," Leon said.

At Christmas 1958, the band found itself in an extraordinary situation. The members liked to be home for Christmas with their families and to play at the M-B Corral for their fans during that time of year.

But Sam had caved in for a good client at the Air Base in Alamogordo and booked The Miller Brothers there over the holidays instead.

"This did not go well at all," Leon said. "The M-B Corral had a crowd; they hired a little old hometown band, probably one out of our agency, anyway they had a full house – and our theory was, why, we must be home on the holidays to show them we appreciate them. But, anyway, this is what broke the camel's back as far as Lee Cochran was concerned."

Lee and Leon had taken almost no time off for years. The hectic pace of touring and playing at the M-B Corral was taking its toll, especially on Lee.

Sam and Leon and Lee talked about the future of The Miller Brothers band, and decided that Lee should join Sam in the office as a member of the booking agency staff.

Why did he want to quit the road?

"Man," said Leon, "he had had his fill."

In addition, by this point in 1959 Leon was tired of the road as well, and it was well known among the music community that he was going to give up the band and also join Sam in the booking agency before too long.

While the group was still regionally popular, mainly west of Wichita Falls, musical tastes of young people were changing, a fact acknowledged by the musical lineup on weekends at the M-B Corral, and the crowd wanting to hear Western Swing was no longer one of younger people. The crowd wanting to hear Western Swing was aging.

"A stable lineup of musicians helped keep the music true to Leon's original vision, but, like Wills, he found himself appealing to a smaller and smaller audience base" (Don Chance 3).

Bobby Rhoades had joined the group in '59 as a fiddle player, and late that year he and his mother made a deal with Leon to buy the band, which essentially meant buying the name and the goodwill, the bus, the uniforms and the booked schedule.

"I had him start renting the rooms, picking up the money, paying the bills, taking the gas in the car, just to get him used to it," Leon said. "And he did. And he was a good man."

Leon was set to leave the band and join the agency early in 1960, but already Lee was telling him that being part of the inside operation was not all it was cracked up to be.

"Lee didn't have a chance," Leon said. "Sam gave him Louisiana, Mississippi, Alabama, Georgia and Florida. Man, that's Bible belt country, and even down when you get past Louisiana, you can book quite a bit of stuff in

Louisiana but not east of it. So Lee stayed, I guess, six months after I came into the agency, and he got with me and said, 'I am getting out of this. I am going to stay with my boys.'"

Lee quit and moved to Fort Worth.

CHAPTER 11

After nearly 30 years of playing music somewhere almost every night of the week, Leon could reflect on a good run as he moved from a career as leader of the band to a career as a booking agent for other musical groups. With The Miller Brothers he had reached the elite ranks in American music. He and the band had become stars, recording artists with at least two fan clubs.

The band got its first national recognition in April of 1955 when *Downbeat Magazine* named The Miller Brothers as "the nation's fastest rising, most exciting Western band in the nation."

In 1956, polls from the Country and Western Jamboree showed Hank Thompson at No. 1 in the big-band category, followed by Pee Wee King at No. 2, and The Miller Brothers at No. 3. The Miller Brothers Trio, a group within the group, was ranked No. 9 among smaller singing outfits.

"Every time a poll came out we were in it somewhere, and our trio was right in there with us," Leon said of that time period.

In July of '56, *Cash Box* had its own poll and asked disc jockeys which band they programmed the most. Hank Thompson ranked first, followed in order by Pee Wee King, Bob Wills, Ray Price, Carl Smith and, at No. 6, The Miller Brothers.

Why would Thompson and Wills and King always rank so high?

"They were good," Leon says, smiling.

Better than The Miller Brothers?

"Yeah," he said. "They had to be, because they

stayed up there. But the label you are on has a lot to do with it, too. Now, Four Star label, the label we were on, seemed like it was good for everyone. Texas Tyler was on it, Miller Brothers, I forget, but quite a few of them. ... It was a good label, but the tunes that you come out with is what really puts you up there. And we just never did get ahold of a tune that was No. 1 material, I guess."

Cash Box in that same year ranked The Miller Brothers as No. 3 in the nation in the Western category, and also named the band "most promising."

Billboard magazine, another national publication, ranked the band at No. 3, as well, that year.

Early in 1957, *Cash Box* ran a feature on The Miller Brothers with their photos and a write-up about their Christmas party at the M-B Corral. In May of that year, *Country and Western Jamboree Magazine* gave good reviews to new releases of the band's old favorites, "Under the Double Eagle" and "Over the Waves." The same magazine ran a poll and the band was voted No. 2 big band in the country and No. 3 big show band in the nation and No. 2 for being the hardest working new band. The magazine invited the band to come to Nashville, Tennessee, for the awards program, but Sam had the boys booked somewhere else and he went himself to accept the honors. This did not sit well with Leon or Lee Cochran, who was showing clear signs of burn-out.

Leon said that he could not understand why they couldn't have some time off, but Sam said they needed to stay hot.

And the band continued to be hot on into 1958.

Cash Box magazine did another poll of disc jockeys to see whose music they used the most, and this time, for the first time, The Miller Brothers beat out Bob Wills and his Texas Playboys.

Hank Thompson was at No. 1, Pee Wee King was at

No. 2, Bill Wimberly was No. 3, and the Miller Brothers were No. 4. Bob Wills was at No. 5.

Ironically, just as it was breaking up in 1959, the band hit its pinnacle.

"They (the magazines) are saying we are No. 3 in the nation," Leon said. "Our trio is No. 4 in the nation. And we are the most versatile dance band in the Western field. Disc jockeys are playing us percentage-wise around third or fourth place. Four Star Records would back up anything we wanted to do."

Some of the songs recorded by Four Star were written by members of The Miller Brothers, and others were written specifically for the group.

One single recorded for Four Star had a Christmas theme and was to be issued right before the season in 1956. On one side of the record was "Happy Birthday, Dear Jesus," and on the other side was a tune called "Rudolph Junior," which was intended to be a take-off on the perennially popular "Rudolph The Red-Nosed Reindeer." The record was released "and was really taking off," Leon said.

It kept rising until Gene Autry, who apparently owned the rights to the original "Rudolph" music, stepped in and asked Four Star to withdraw the record or face a lawsuit.

The last tune recorded by The Miller Brothers with Leon as its leader was one Leon wrote with his daughter Carole, sitting at the piano at his home in Wichita Falls.

"She'd sit at the piano," Leon said, "and I'd hum this song, sing the words, she'd put in the chords, and I'd tell her, 'No, put in so-and-so.'"

Carole, however, remembered the situation this way:

"I was on the piano, and you were on the fiddle. I didn't do much more than chord, so you wrote most of it."

The song was called "Today, Tomorrow and From Now On," and Carole was listed with Leon as composer when the record came out.

"It did pretty good," Leon said, then amending himself, added, "It did real good. ... It was a five-star song, a new hit as an all-new song."

Interestingly, Carole recalled receiving a royalty check from the music company one time. It was for $1.68.

Actually, Leon said, smiling, his daughter never got any of the checks that came in the form of royalty payments; those all came to him.

"I guess I do owe her some money now, don't I?" he grinned.

As Leon reflected back on the music and the band after the turn of the century, he wasn't analytical or critical.

When asked if there were a major difference between what The Miller Brothers were singing and writing and what Hank Thompson and Bob Wills were singing and writing, he said, "Not really. Not really. But, if I were the one who was passing out those awards, Hank Thompson would have been first, music-wise. As far as putting everything together, Pee Wee King would have been second. And I'll go along with the disc jockeys; we would have been third. We would take the simplest little old song and put an arrangement on it, an intro, and then play the song exactly the way it was released, because they asked you for a song and that's the way they wanted to hear it, and we'd have to put an ending on it. And as far as music was concerned, I don't believe there was ever a band that knew what they were doing more than us. Because we knew the rules. We knew why we were doing this. We knew why you needed certain chords there. And we played classical, we played everything under the sun."

Was it, then, simply a matter of getting a break on a particular song that caught the public's fancy?

"A matter of getting a break, and your record company," he said.

And part of making it to No. 1 was being in the right place at the right time. Twice the band members were asked to physically move to Nashville, to be closer to the music scene, and twice they refused because of the M-B Corral and because they wanted to be in Wichita Falls where their families were.

"The Miller Brothers never quite caught on with fans the way so many other outfits did," Don Chance has written. "Why? Who knows? Even today, last year's Grammy winner could well be this year's 'where-are-they-now' joke."

Chance does, though, speculate on some factors:

While Bob Wills was an extremely well-respected, prize-winning old-time fiddler and stylistic innovator, most everyone who worked with the Miller Brothers and the Texas Playboys agrees that Leon Gibbs was an equally gifted innovator, and by far the better musician. Also, while Wills always surrounded himself with flashy, supremely accomplished fiddle players, Leon always led his various lineups as the primary (and also supremely accomplished) fiddler. Both formulas are proven to work equally well.

That Bob Wills began recording before the Miller Brothers might have something to do with the Texas Playboys eventually emerging as the better-known group. Before World War II, recordings were used mainly as marketing tools for personal appearances. Most successful groups also had live radio shows, which were almost guaranteed to drum up interest in local dance bookings, and both the Miller Brothers and Bob Wills used their respective radio programs to promote all their live performances. But with records as calling cards, artists could also get their music to other radio stations for possible airplay whenever they were booked to play distant road gigs, and not have to show up to play live on the air.

Even so, neither outfit could know, at the time they recorded them, the impact, if any, their records would have on the future. In fact, as Leon Rausch insists, such groups as the Miller Brothers and Bob Wills were often forced to adapt their sounds to changing trends as popular musical tastes evolved – especially during the musically volatile 50s. (Chance 2)

The legacy of the Miller Brothers can be looked at another way, and that has to do with the influence the band had over the years on the direction of country music and the development of musicians. Even after Western Swing had become more or less a regional sound for an aging audience, the influence remained strong.

"Without the sweet-toned twin-fiddle sound favored by Ray Price, another Texas-born artist who readily credits Leon Gibbs with shaping his early musical tastes, there probably would have been no 'Nashville Sound' as developed in the 1960s," Chance said, adding,

Without vocalist Tommy Duncan, who toured and recorded with both the Texas Playboys and the Miller Brothers there likely would have been no Waylon Jennings. Without steel guitarist Leon McAuliffe, who also worked for both groups, Lloyd Maines might not have taken up the steel, putting him in the position to encourage his daughter, Natalie, into the musical career that led to her taking over the lead singing chores with the Dixie

Chicks.

When Asleep at the Wheel emerged in the mid-1970s as a quirky and popular throwback to the Western Swing of the 1940s, even most lifelong country fans assumed that the Wheel sound was rooted in the musical legacy of the Texas Playboys. But Wheel founder and leader Ray Benson has often cited the Miller Brothers, alongside Wills, as his primary influences. The Asleep at the Wheel discography clearly shows this in the fact that, though the group has produced several Bob Wills tribute albums, some of them winning Grammy Awards, most of the Wheel's recorded output is noticeably short on original Texas Playboys material while including subtle stylistic elements (such as the boogie-woogie piano riffs) originated by Leon Gibbs' various bands.

George Strait, Mark Chesnutt, Tracy Byrd, the Dixie Chicks, Garth Brooks, most successful Texas- and Oklahoma-born country artists include at least one Western Swing-flavored number on every new album, and all seem to strive for the exacting stylistic authenticity of the late 1940s. (Chance 3)

Of course, there would have been country music without the influences of the Miller Brothers and the Texas Playboys.

"But would the music swing as infectiously?" Chance asked. "I doubt it."

The legacy of the band can also be looked at in still another way, and that way is summed up in another anecdote from Leon:

"A guy in Jackson Hole, Wyoming, one time told Sam, he said, 'Sam, [The Miller Brothers] may not be No. 1, but in my book they are No. 1. They are the finest bunch of men, the hardest bunch of working boys I ever saw in my life,' and he said, 'They treated every customer like they were something special.'"

CHAPTER 12

When he joined the Sam Gibbs Orchestral Service in early 1960, Leon said he figured it would be a good fit for him and his personality. He liked being out meeting new people and greeting people he'd met in the music business, and he didn't mind being on the road. His territory was West Texas, New Mexico, Arizona and California, and he already knew many of the club and bar owners because The Miller Brothers had for years performed in those states.

A booking agency represents bands on tour, and Leon went to the clubs and bars to get signed contracts, making sure to coordinate with a master schedule maintained in Wichita Falls at the agency offices.

He enjoyed the job for about six years, and never really played much during that time because he was so busy on the road. In that sixth year, though, he got an offer he didn't really want to refuse. Jimmie Davis was running for governor of Louisiana again, and he wanted Leon to join a band he was putting together to make another tour of the state.

Leon was gone for three weeks on the Louisiana tour with what Davis called The Sunshine Boys, and during that time Sam was supposed to keep Leon's tours up to date out West. When Leon got back, he hit the road again because some of the groups he represented needed dates to play to fill out their tour schedules.

For two straight days, he said he called the agency office to get updates on schedules and never could get an answer. On the third day, he did get through to Sam, who told him that all the dates he had scheduled had already been filled and he would have to cancel them.

Leon hurried home.

"So I came in and he was just having a fit," Leon said. "I had stood about all of this I wanted to, really. I was kind of like Lee (Cochran); I was whipped and wore out. I wanted to come in anyway. So, he said, 'You are going to have to cancel every one of these.' I said, 'No, you are going to cancel them.'"

In the end, Leon wound up selling all of his part of the business and a property rental business to Sam for $747, an amount he hit on quickly just to get away from it all.

"My wife said, 'You are an idiot, but I love you and I am glad you quit.'"

About the same time Leon had his falling out with Sam, the new version of The Miller Brothers was also falling apart.

Leon had been booking the band out West so he could keep up with what was going on with the outfit under Bobby Rhoades, the band member who had bought The Miller Brothers when Leon had decided to quit.

"Bobby Rhoades for some reason started messing up," Leon said. "People didn't like it. Gene quit using him at the M-B Corral."

The band had been playing the Golden Nugget in Las Vegas and lost that contract, too. And then he started losing his best players. Frankie McWhorter went with Bob Wills, and the steel guitar player left, as did Dutch Ingram, longtime drummer.

Ultimately, Rhoades' mother, who actually paid for the band, sold the group to Johnny Patterson, another musician who had played off and on with The Miller Brothers.

The end of the musical trail for The Miller Brothers came in 1962. While Patterson still owns the name, there was no Western Swing band known as The Miller Brothers going into the new century.

After leaving the agency, Leon said he kind of lost his head:

"When I first got out of the agency, I was about 20-something years behind on drinking. And this is the truth. So I don't know why, but my wife said, 'What are you going to do?' and I said, 'I don't know. I'm going to catch up on my drinking. And just down-right ignorance and a fool — I wanted to catch up, I guess. And I did.'"

Leon didn't quit playing during this time, although he did do a lot of drinking. He recalled, however, working some with Kenny Brewer and with some other, smaller combos.

Before long, though, he was contacted again by Jimmie Davis, who wanted Leon to be a permanent member of his campaign band, the Sunshine Boys.

Leon moved to Louisiana, where he found Davis as good a friend as he'd ever had. All expenses were paid, and they stayed in the finest hotels, and on weekends, Leon would come home. He stayed with Davis for a year.

"There was not a town or not a county – parish, they call it – that we missed going through," Leon said. "We went through every little old town. We may not have spoke there, but lots of times we'd stop and be hot and drink a cold beer or something. And it was a good deal. And what made it so good, man, I had a brand new Chevy, and I had a credit card, and anything – if you wanted to take somebody, they'd want it to be *somebody*, to dinner, you'd just pick up the tab and they gave you the money. It beat anything I ever saw."

The year was a whirlwind.

"We played dances and parties on oil barges in Louisiana," he said. "They have big parties. And shrimp – oh man, they'd put on a feed. And we'd play. No set hours.

They furnished the drinks, they furnished the food. And there was never any money involved in this thing. That was just all included in your deal, and we enjoyed it. And we always enjoyed Bourbon Street. We rode the street cars. I played a hospital with Jimmie Davis, and it was a leper colony. All people there had leprosy, and, man, I was afraid to touch anything. And, lo and behold, I looked out there when we were leaving, and there was Jimmie Davis shaking hands with every soul that left that building."

Leon remembered recording one song with Davis during that period. It was for the Decca label (Davis had been the first personality to record for Decca when the label started in 1934).

They flew in a Piper Cub to Nashville, Tennessee. "It came the darndest storm you ever saw," he said. "And this old boy's radio wouldn't work, and he said, 'Hey, guys, help me look for that airport.' And, we got there and we recorded the song, we got in that plane and went back and we started out and played four jobs that day."

After the election, Leon was offered a state job if he'd stick around in Louisiana, but he was ready to come home and so was his wife.

Back home, he played with the MB Trio, which included Madge Bolin on piano and Emory Mussiel on drums and Leon on fiddle. They played every Tuesday night at the Red Door senior citizens center in Wichita Falls.

In 1966, Bob Wills sold The Texas Playboys to Carl Johnson of Fort Worth, a man who had been in the trucking business but was a big fan of the band.

A year later, Johnson called Leon and asked if he would come work for the Playboys and Johnson and book the band.

Leon joined up just to run things, and not to play

in the band. That meant he could stay close to home. But after about a year, the band members persuaded Leon to take up his fiddle and get back on stage with them, and he did.

"Man, you talk about work," he said. "Booking it, playing it and talking to (Johnson) every morning at 8 o'clock for an hour was really a job. (Johnson had the habit of calling Leon to find out what had gone on the night before, and the call always came at 8 a.m.) Now, it paid. And he never questioned any money you spent."

In fact, Johnson complained on occasion because Leon was not spending enough money, particularly on phone calls to and dinners for disc jockeys and club owners. It was supposed to be part of Leon's job to schmooze with the decision-makers.

"One month we had a kind of slow month . . .Carl called me one morning, said, 'Man, Gibbs, what happened?' Said, 'Your phone bill's way off this month.' Said, 'You are not calling anybody.' So I went home and told Cleo, told my wife, I said, 'Phone everybody you can think of – call your uncle in Denton, call your uncle in Denver. Phone everybody, just make a bunch of calls to anybody anywhere.' She did, and the phone bill went up. And I just hit it lucky, and we had a really big month the next month. So, he said, 'You see what happens when you're working, Gibbs?' 'Yeah,' I said, 'it pays off, Carl.'"

Some things, however, Leon would not do for Johnson and the Playboys.

"Carl wanted me to go to Nashville, meet some people and push and get Leon Rausch a hit," he said. "I said, 'Carl, I can't do that.'

"'Hey, if you've got enough money you can.' He said, 'I am talking about going down there and take these people out. Wine and dine them. Give them Leon's record. Be on their program'."

"I said, 'Carl, I don't want to do that.' I didn't want to do that. 'What you are doing is kind of blackmailing.' But if you look back, I know now where he got his idea. See, along about that time there was a big stink about people buying hits. ...'"

Several times during the 50s and 60s, Nashville and Memphis and other recording centers were rocked by scandals when it was revealed that record companies were paying disc jockies to give preferential treatment to their stars and their stars' work.

At length, the pace of touring again with a band took a toll on Leon, and when he found one of the band members had lied about stealing a case of beer, he used the handling of the situation as a reason to quit.

"It gave me an excuse for getting away," he said. "Certain things would absolutely kill you. And I'd had enough of those things. Not only had I had enough of this, my first wife had had enough of this – so we get a divorce."

Leon blames himself for the breakup.

"Now, she was a wonderful woman," he said. "I do not have one thing in the world to say against her. I cannot praise any woman as much as her, unless it's my wife now. I praise her this much.

"But I got hard to get along with. Even harder than I had been."

When Carl Johnson came to Wichita Falls to try to get Leon to come back with the Playboys, he refused.

"And I was really drinking then, because my wife had quit me, and I was just fooling around, more or less just wasting time and money," he said.

But not for long.

One day he got a call from Woodrow Hare, a long-time acquaintance who had moved to Roswell, New Mexico. Hare wanted Leon to move there to join him in a venture he knew would make them some money. Hare wanted Leon to partner up with him to buy the liquor license owned by a man who had been running a place just outside Roswell called Scotty's Place.

Leon agreed, moved to Roswell, borrowed the money to buy his part of the license, and they set up shop, opening up only three nights a week. The license cost them $60,000.

"Well, we had the crowds," Leon said. "Admission was free – 200 people. We'd fill that place up as full as a tick. It would be full. And beer was 75 cents then. Your best whiskey was $1.25. And your cheaper whiskey was $1 a shot."

Right away, Leon put a band together that played the three nights the club was open. He led the group and, of course, played fiddle, but the group never played anywhere else and he never even gave it a name.

During this period, his wife was still with him, although the marriage was shaky, and she took care of the beverage sales.

Leon, however, found out quickly that running a nightclub was very different from working in one.

"There's two old boys there, known drunkards, and the bartender had poured them a drink," he said. "They called me over there and said, 'Wherever we go they set the bottle up here and we pour our own drinks.' I said, 'Well, man, I'd be happy to if I could afford it, but I can't.' 'Well, hell, everybody else does.' Said, 'What if I get up here and walked on this counter?' I said, 'It sure would hurt my business, fella.' And my wife came up and she was in charge of the bar, and I said (for some reason, I don't know how this happened, but word got out, and I started it, I guess, that she was a karate expert – judo, black belt), I called her over there, and I said, 'Hon, now, I've told you and told you, don't ever use your karate and your judo, and don't show off your black belt. Now, I've told you this, but these two right here, if they get smart with you, give them your best shot.'

"The old boy looked at me – I said, 'Hey, no problem, man. She's not going to bother you unless I tell her to. And then she's going to knock hell plumb out of you when she gets at you.'

"I don't know how come I said that.

"Did you know, the guys drank their drinks, they paid their bill and they left and they never did come back."

Leon never did hire any security for the club and never did have much trouble after that incident.

The people who owned the place before he and Woody bought it had at one time barred one "old drunk" from ever coming back to the place. He decided to test the new owners, so the fellow called Leon up one day and announced that he'd be coming to the club that evening.

"I said, 'Hey, man, I am not the one you need to talk to. Call the police, tell them that you want to come out here and you are going to straighten up.' And he said, 'Hell, I ain't going to come out there and just kinda tear the place up. I am going out there and stab you.'"

Leon thought he might be able to bluff the man.

"I said, 'You are always talking about what you are going to do, and you never do it. I don't want your business in the first place. I don't want you out here. But if you are going to come out here, I want you to tear this thing up so I can collect some insurance. Now, don't just come out here and piddle around. Do something.'"

The man never did show up.

After about two years of the co-ownership, Woody got sick and died, and his wife did not want to continue with the partnership.

She and Leon sold their license for $85,000, a tidy profit.

By this point, Cleo was ready to leave for good, and Leon split part of the profits with her so she could return to Wichita Falls.

No sooner had the deal closed than Leon heard from Carl Johnson. This time Carl did not want Leon to run the Texas Playboys. He had bought the Reo Palm Isle Club in Longview, Texas, and wanted Leon to come work with the band, which was much like the old Miller Brothers.

The Reo Palm Isle was bigger than the M-B Corral and stayed open six nights a week with a matinee from 4 p.m. to 7 p.m. on Wednesdays and Sundays. The band would rehearse new music after closing time on Thursdays.

A long list of celebrities found their way to the Reo Palm Isle Club – Brenda Lee, Ray Price, Willie Nelson, Waylon Jennings, Hank Thompson. The music was almost always country.

After his divorce, Leon met and fell for a woman named Audrey Wright, and he would travel home to Wichita Falls as often as he could to see her. After he'd been with Johnson's club for about five months, he asked for an extra day or two off so he and Audrey could fly to Las Vegas and get married. Then, back in Longview, they lived in the apartment Leon had rented, made friends and enjoyed East Texas. But when Leon's contract was up, he and Audrey were ready to come back to Wichita Falls.

"Carl said, 'If you ever want to come back, you don't even have to call,'" Leon said. "He said, 'Just show up. Just be sure you are on time.'"

In Wichita Falls now, Leon began playing at the M-B Corral again a couple of nights a week. He also played for other special events.

At the M-B Corral, he played with Jimmy Boggs, who he called "the finest guitar man I've ever heard anywhere."

Before long, though, Jimmie Davis was on the phone again, asking Leon to come back to Louisiana to help the former governor get elected to another term. Leon needed the money, so he reluctantly agreed to rejoin the Davis tour. He traveled back and forth between Wichita Falls and whatever point he was to start from in Louisiana, and kept up that pace for about a year, but this time Davis lost the election.

When Leon got back to Wichita Falls, he said he realized how tired he was, and he and Audrey talked about him getting out of the music business altogether. Ultimately, that's what they decided to do.

"She was tickled to death, actually," Leon said, "because she was afraid something else would come up out of town. I decided I was going to quit playing, and I folded that fiddle up and put it under the bed and didn't touch it for two years. Did not play a lick. Everyone called and wanted me to work. Finally, they all stopped calling because they knew I wouldn't."

Instead, Leon sought a job at a department store in Wichita Falls called Gibson's, which he obtained, thanks to his nephew Bobby Gibbs, who was an executive in the Gibson's chain of retail outlets. He got the job, becoming head of the sporting goods department at the Gibson's in downtown Wichita Falls.

While he could sell, he had no idea how to buy for his department, but he quickly learned that the sporting goods manager at the other Wichita Falls store, located on Kell Boulevard in the western part of the city, knew what he was doing.

"Boy, when he bought so many gross of golf balls, I bought half of that," Leon said, noting that the downtown store's sales volume was about one-half that of the Kell Boulevard store. "I don't care what he bought, I bought just about half of it. It never turned out so perfect for not knowing nothing – I mean, nothing. I just bought half of what he did."

A short time later, Leon was put in charge of all Gibson's advertising.

While Leon was doing well in a new career, even doing things in new ways wasn't saving the M-B Corral. Scheduling rock 'n' roll musicians on a regular basis didn't allow the Wagners, who had bought out Leon and the other club owners, to keep the place going. They sold the building to the Veterans of Foreign Wars for a post home, and the VFW stayed in the facility into the 21st century, although it was already listed as being for sale in 2002.

At the same time the Corral was going out of business, Leon got back into show business in a big, if short-lived, way when Peter Bogdanovich needed a band to play some scenes in his movie written by Larry McMurtry called *The Last Picture Show*.

Leon played fiddle and led the group, and Jimmy Boggs played guitar and was vocalist, Grady Soloman played guitar and was a vocalist, Bob Lemley was on bass, and Jesse Marino was on drums. For their scenes, the group set up at the American Legion Hall and on a flatbed truck in Archer City on the square.

"They would have us playing a song and everyone would dance," he said. "They'd have us stop playing and make the motion that you are playing, and then this Peter Bogdanovich with a loudspeaker would say, 'Don't bunch up,' and they'd keep dancing, see, and he would say, 'Do it again.' We'd start off a song to give them the tempo they were going to dance to, and then he'd say, 'Get closer together.' And just on and on. ..."

Their scenes were shot on film over five nights. Then the group's music was actually recorded at the American Legion Hall, with the band trying to match the tempo of what they'd been acting like they were playing during the filming of the scene.

"They paid everybody – listen to this – everybody got paid the next morning, cash," Leon said. "I've never seen anything, never heard of anything like it. And we got double scale. Almost double. We got California musicians' scale, which was at least half more than ours."

Later, when Bogdanovich shot the sequel to *The Last Picture Show* in Archer City and Wichita Falls, Leon was recruited to play again. For that movie, called *Texasville*, Leon pulled in members of band that regularly played at the J Bar Corral, a nightclub in Wichita Falls, and the musical scenes were shot in much the same way. The band would "fake" playing while scenes were being shot and then redo the music later, trying to get the tempo and starts and stops just right.

Pursuing his non-musical career, Leon stayed in the retail business for about another year when he heard from his brother Sam. The two brothers had not spoken to each other for more than two years.

"Of course, we made up from our fuss," Leon said. "Like brothers, we fell out, and like brothers, we made up. Like you're supposed to."

Sam wanted Leon to teach lessons at night at the Sam Gibbs Music Co. store. "I wanted to do it," Leon said. "I hadn't been playing for maybe five years, and my music was just at a standstill."

No sooner had he started teaching than demand for him to teach picked up, and he started thinking about just devoting full time to giving lessons.

"So, I told Audrey, 'Lord have mercy, I am going to quit – I've quit traveling, I've quit playing, but I enjoyed teaching.'"

Since he had not taught before in a formal way, Leon asked Sam to give him only beginning students at first, even on the fiddle, but especially on guitar since that was not his first instrument.

"I looked at the music books, and I knew everything they did, only now I was brushing up on the 'why' of what I did," he said.

CHAPTER 13

When Leon quit Gibson's Discount Stores to teach full-time in a one-on-one studio at Sam Gibbs Music Co., he had with him 50 years of experience playing fiddle, singing and leading a band.

But he'd never really played guitar, and he had to brush up on that and mandolin, to be able to teach as many instruments and pupils as possible.

When word got out that Leon was teaching, he found himself with a waiting list. He would take on all comers, from preschoolers with a natural talent to aging Baby Boomers who wanted to learn how to read music and play guitar for their grandkids, from no-talents to super talents.

One of those who showed up was Jack Stevens, a man known around the Wichita Falls area for his artwork and sculptures. The last of 14 kids, Jack grew up without any formal musical training. He said that after his parents moved into a tent in 1936 near Holliday Creek in Wichita Falls, his dad would pull out his fiddle, and one brother would pull out a mandolin, and he'd strum along on an old guitar. Over time, of course, his parents died, his siblings scattered, and Jack never thought much about making music. He was too busy being a cowboy, a farmer and an artist.

But after his dad died one of his sisters brought him the old man's fiddle, a copy of a 1721 Stradivarius. Then his oldest son gave him, as a Christmas present, a gift certificate for three months worth of lessons with Leon Gibbs.

"He has been so patient with me trying to learn to

play the fiddle," Jack wrote in a short memoir. "It ain't nothing like keeping time with a guitar. At first, I thought something was wrong with Papa's fiddle since it is so old or maybe sure-nuff something was wrong with the bow. But when I told that to Mr. Gibbs, he took it and went to playing 'Amazing Grace' on it. It was so beautiful, and the sound so full and mellow, it vibrated your chest. I learned not to blame them squeaks on the fiddle any more. Took full blame myself."

In his lessons with Leon, Jack began learning the old hymns and religious tunes he had heard on those evenings in the Great Depression outside the family tent near Holliday Creek.

"Mr. Gibbs has been able to play any tune that I could remember and a lot of them I didn't remember," Jack wrote. "I'm really grateful that I wound up with Papa's fiddle. It means so much to me. But I am also so glad I have been able to take lessons from Mr. Gibbs. The sounds he makes on his fiddle (I should say, violin, 'cause Papa always told me the difference between a violin and a fiddle was, a violin you carry in a case, a fiddle you carry in a toe-sack. Mr. Gibbs has a case, and Papa's came to me in a case, so they are both violins.). When Mr. Gibbs plays, his sounds like a violin. When I play Papa's violin, it sounds like it's a cross between a homemade fiddle and one of them foreign bagpipes."

Jack said he's enjoyed visiting with Leon as much as he's enjoyed learning how to play the fiddle. "He has the same biblical convictions that I do, and he plays all the old church songs," Jack wrote. "When he plays harmony with me on Papa's violin, it even makes my playing sound good. ... If I was a sure-enough good player, which I ain't, I'd still want to take lessons from Mr. Gibbs. He's not only a good player, he has a good outlook on life. I just enjoy being with him, hearing him play music."

Another friend who said he learned a lot from Leon, though not in a formal sense, is David Holcomb, a gifted musician and teacher who came to find out about Leon's talent in a rather circuitous way.

Back in the 60s, David was a hot guitar player for a band called The Misfits. Their leader contacted Sam Gibbs Orchestra Service to book the group into jobs in the general area of Wichita Falls.

"We knew Sam had a booking agency and that he handled several of the groups working on the road," David recalled. "We also were aware of his connection to The Miller Brothers band and that he booked Bob Wills. Our understanding was that Sam did the bookings while Leon worked out on the road contacting club managers and getting the groups lined out to play. That was good enough for us. All we had to do was show up, perform and pay our agents their percentage of the pay – the rest was profit.

"During this time we saw Sam on a regular basis, but Leon was the 'mystery man.' We never saw him or met him. We just knew that he was putting in a good word for us and helping us working."

The band, however, broke up a little later when some members went into the military, and others went to college.

"Now, jump ahead 12 or so years to the late 70s," David wrote. "College had been completed, military obligations done. I was happily married, and learning to use those music skills in a new way as an orchestra teacher.

"One day, one of my high school students asked if I knew the tune 'Maiden's Prayer' because his private teacher (Leon) had shown him how to play it. I had heard the tune before, but at that time, not being well grounded in Western Swing, I really couldn't offer much in return. This did, however, pique my interest, so I started listening to 'fiddle music,' trying to pick up a few tunes here and there. After all, you never know when something might come in handy and, as a kid I had played violin in the school orchestra. I had secretly wanted to fiddle but didn't know anyone to show me how."

Since several of his students were taking fiddle lessons from Leon, David figured it might be a good idea to meet the mystery man. "Leon probably doesn't know this, but when we 'formally' met, I came away thinking about what a genuinely nice guy he was," David wrote. "He spent the time (as I later found to be so much his character) complimenting the students we shared and also me as a teacher – that's Leon."

Over the years, David said he found Leon to be an excellent coach. And he cited as an example one student who came to David's high-school program from junior high school as a talented violinist with a reputation as a kid who was aiming to be a star. His name was Kyle Aaron Lopez.

While Kyle had talent (David called him "the human tape recorder" because his ear for music was so good) and ambition, he had limited experience and didn't read music as well as other students.

"This presented a somewhat serious situation since most students in the high-school orchestra have been playing at least four years and are proficient at note reading," David wrote. "After talking with Leon, we decided that our strategy would be for him to work on the fiddle aspects and for me to help develop the reading skills because the kid was already talking about becoming a professional musician."

Together they worked with Kyle, and his reading skills improved, as did his "fiddle" skills, and he went on to win various competitions. He was soon honing his talent further in college.

"Leon and I just look up and smile," David wrote.

"Thanks (to) Leon for encouraging Kyle and for setting him on a course that promises great things as he continues his career in music."

Leon's proud of most of his students, but one of those he's proudest of is Brooke Whyrick, who started taking violin lessons from him when she was only four years old.

"She is a born genius," he said. "The most remarkable child I have ever seen in my life."

At the time, she was already playing at nursing homes and at churches. And she was already dreaming big, according to her grandmother, who said: "Brooke's little 16th fiddle is on a shelf. Also on that shelf is a little wish box that Mr. Gibbs gave her. Every once in awhile I let her get it down and listen to the little tune it plays. And in that wish box is a wish that she can play as well as Mr. Gibbs someday."

Another student came to classes with Leon lugging church hymns that had been set to guitar music for a folk choir, and each of the songs required dozens of chord changes, some involving chords that were very hard to play one right after another in progression, a challenge to even the most adept guitar picker.

Working through the music methodically, humming the melodies to himself and picking note to note and chord to chord, Leon helped the student simplify the passages so even a relative novice could play the tunes without bobbling. Even in his early 80s, Leon's able to remember tunes and words to songs he hasn't actually played in years.

In the fall of 2002, he began playing for three hours one Saturday night per month at the Senior Citizens Center in Petrolia, Texas, about 17 miles northeast of Wichita Falls.

The center's jamboree nights drew about 100 each

Saturday to listen as musicians with a widely varying range of skills tried their hand at old country and gospel favorites.

Before Leon's discovery of the center show, the band on any given Saturday night might include as many as a half-dozen guitar players and a bass man or two but no fiddle players at all.

Leon's fiddling added a dimension of an unexpected sort when he started showing up with an electrified violin and amplifier in hand.

He never required even a look at the musical scores when dozens and dozens of songs were offered up and performed by the assembled players, and the songs ranged from old Jimmie Davis numbers to Patsy Cline to, of course, Bob Wills and The Texas Playboys.

As purely and sweetly as if they were coming from Leon's fiddle 50 years before, the notes soared above the strumming guitars and bumping bass, making you wish the songs would go on forever.

Leon's so adept at his trade that if you can hum a few bars to a new tune, he can write out the rest of it because he knows the rules music works by.

A student who knew more about rhyming words than he did about making music once wrote a couple of songs for Leon to look at and critique. One was supposed to be a blues number, written in typical 12-bar blues style with the standard blues progression of chords in the key of A.

As Leon tried to play what the student had written, he found himself strumming a different beat pattern.

"Why," he said, with an encouraging note of pleasure and surprise in his voice, "you have written a nice waltz here!"

CHAPTER 14

In 2001, Leon Gibbs turned 80. He was still teaching, but he wasn't playing much. He and Audrey, however, did enjoy going every Friday night to Archer City to listen to a group called The Over The Hill Band, which played some of the old Western Swing tunes that Leon helped popularize with The Miller Brothers.

The band consisted of Wally Hendrixson, the leader and steel guitar player; bass player Hank Whitson; Mickey Dan Stoddard on drums and trumpet; Jimmy Vie on guitar; and Frank Farnsworth on fiddle.

The Over The Hill Band began talking early in the year about throwing a whing-ding in celebration of Leon's birthday that would truly be his "Last Fling" on stage as a fiddle player and band leader.

The Last Fling was scheduled for April 20, and was a sell-out.

At this Last Fling, Leon said, "David Holcomb came out and played with us, and Kyle Aaron … came out and stole the show – absolutely stole the show." But everyone really turned out to make this Last Fling special for Leon.

A couple of months later, Leon and Sam Gibbs were inducted into the Legends of Western Swing Hall of Fame during a Western Swing festival held in Wichita Falls that featured, among many others, the Texas Playboys.

Then in November of 2001, Leon was asked to play for one day during the grand reopening of the Kell House Museum. The museum had been closed for renovations, and the grand reopening featured an exhibit called "The History of Music and Musical Instruments, 1900-1950."

Leon played fiddle with David Holland on guitar, and also answered visitors' questions about The Miller Brothers and fiddle playing. From the get-go, Leon was nervous about performing in such an intimate setting. After all, he hadn't really played much for the public since "retiring."

When the doors opened, about 25 people came right in the front door.

"The first people that walked in was a 94-year-old woman and her daughter," Leon recalled. "And she said, 'Why, Leon Miller, I'd know you anywhere.' Said, 'You haven't changed a bit.' And that made me feel real good, and she said, 'What was that waltz you recorded?' Said, 'I remember dancing it at the M-B Corral.' So, I said, 'We recorded 'Wednesday Night Waltz' and "Over the Waves.' 'Over the Waves,' she said. So I just turned around and I told David, 'waltz,' and I turned right to her and I played 'Over the Waves' and, man, the crowd, about 20 or 25 of them, just settled in and everybody started talking."

Leon enjoyed answering questions about the bands he played with and the M-B Corral, and he played whatever the crowd requested, from "Faded Love" to "Wild Side of Life," and dozens more.

Before the end of 2001 it was apparent that the 2001 "Last Fling" was not actually to be his last fling. Leon was still teaching on an almost full-time basis, and was playing here and there when he could. The Over the Hill Band, among others, was talking about doing a "Second Last Fling" in April 2002.

Again, it was a sold-out crowd that gathered on April 27, 2002, for Leon's "Second Last Fling" featuring the Over the Hill Band.

Before the lights were dimmed in the huge Knights of Columbus Hall on Turtle Creek Road in Wichita Falls, Leon made his way from table to table talking to students and longtime fans.

One young woman related that she'd been taking guitar lessons from Leon for less than a year. After she'd been taking for about five months, she said, she asked Leon if he "was going to hang in there with me."

"He said, 'Honey, I'm 80. I'll do what I can,'" she said.

Before getting behind the microphone, Leon, dressed in an olive drab shirt, with black vest with a brown cowboy hat on his head, confided: "Needless to say, I'm a nervous wreck."

But that's not, of course, the way he appeared when he had his fiddle in his hand.

"A big Western howdy to you folks," he began as the lights faded. "Some of you I've known for a long time. Some take you way, way back. … We will play some slow, some fast and some half-fast. Here we go. Let's hit the dance floor."

Throughout the night, Leon took requests "for anything" and played them.

Under blue, green and yellow lights, he leaned forward to hear what fans wanted him to play, and some were as old as he was.

Kyle Aaron Lopez was there, and he played several tunes, including a duet on "Faded Love" with Leon.

And then, before midnight, it was over.

Will there be another – a "Third Last Fling?"

"I hope so," Leon said, folding up his fiddle case and pushing the cowboy hat back on his head.

APPENDIX ONE:
DISCOGRAPHY

Neither Leon Gibbs nor anyone else associated with the Miller Brothers Band kept a complete discography of the band's recordings over the years. However, a group of music fans in Europe did track down as much information as they could compile back in the 1980s and published a discography in a newsletter. Leon Gibbs has examined their work and believes it is complete and accurate. The credit for this compilation goes to Phillip J. Tricker, Ray Topping, Dick Grant, Keith Kolby, Henri Laffont and someone called "Big Al."

When published in the newsletter, the compilers added this note: "In view of the complex nature of 4 Star releases, the discography has been set out with matrix numbers at the left. Releases have been split into three columns – Regular, Specials and ETs.

				Regular	Specials	ETs
MILLER BROS. ORCHESTRA		Circa late '40s				
103;	"My Baby Girl"	Vo-Jay Starnes DELTA	103/104			
104;	"Shanty Town"	Vo-Band	———	———		
TOMMY DUNCAN AND MILLER BROS. BAND		Cliff Herring Studio, Fort Worth, Texas				
FW 2018 X	"I Guess You Were Right"	Vo-Tommy Duncan	INTRO	6071	16 March 1953	
FW 2020 Q	"Hound Dog"	Vo- ———				
FW 2016 X	"Stars Over San Antone"	Vo- ——— ———	INTRO	6080		
FW 2017 Q	"I Reckon I'm a Texan"	Vo- ———				
FW 2019 X	"The Tennessee Churchbells"	Vo- ——— ———	INTRO	6086		
FW 2021 Q	"That Uncertain Feeling"	Vo- ———				
BILL TAYLOR		Fort Worth, Texas (?) '53				
6426	"Yo Yo Heart"	Vo- Bill Taylor	4 STAR	1650	X 80	ET 118
6427	"One of Your Lies"	Vo- ———			—— ——	
MILLER BROS. BAND (Recording dates unknown but are between 1954 and 1963)						
6553	"Rose of Tijuana"	Vo- Billy Thompson	4 STAR		X 88	ET 123
6554	"That's How Long I Love You"	Vo- ———			—— ——	
	"New Potato Stomp"	Instrumental	4 STAR			ET 124
	"Tuning the Fiddle"	—————	4 STAR			ET 125
	"Express Polka"	—————	4 STAR			125
6555	"Today, Tomorrow and From Now On"	Vo- Thompson	4 STAR	1667	P 103	ET 126
6556 (?)	"Nursery Rhyme Blues"	Vo- Billy Thompson	4 STAR	——	——	
	"Woodchuck Boogie"	Instrumental 4 STAR				ET 129
6742	"Fiddlin' Stomp"	—————	4 STAR	1673	P 104	ET 131
6743	"Geronimo"	Vo- Dutch Ingram	4 STAR	——	——	
6793	"Trailway Blues"	Vo- Billy Taylor	4 STAR	1678		133
6794	"Broken-Hearted Girl"	Vo- ———	4 STAR	——		——
	"Denver Hop"	Instrumental 4 STAR		1680		ET 134
	"Alligator Rag"	—————	4 STAR	——		124

6792	"As You Were Standing By My Side"	Vo- Billy Thompson	4 STAR	1683	ET	135
6795	"Tulsa Baby"	Vo- Billy Taylor	4 STAR	——		——
	"Travelin'"	Instrumental 4 STAR			ET	136
	"Rambling Around"	———————	4 STAR			——
6840	"Happy Birthday, Dear Jesus"	Vo- Billy Thompson	4 STAR	1686		
6841	"Rudolph Junior"	Vo- —— —————	4 STAR	——		
	"Water Baby Blues"	Instrumental	4 STAR		ET	137
	"Stepping It Off"	———————	4 STAR			——
6865	"Hey, Pretty Baby"	Vo- Lee Miller 4 STAR		1694	ET	138
6868	"Who's Gonna Know?"	Vo- Billy Thompson	4 STAR	——		——
6877	"Loco Choo Choo"	Vo- Jimmy McGraw	4 STAR	1699		
6878	"Why Must It Be?"	Vo- ——————	4 STAR			
6885	"Over The Waves"	Instrumental 4 STAR	1702			
6888	"Under the Double Eagle"	———————	4 STAR	——		
6884	"The Triflin' Kind"	Vo- Jimmy McGraw	4 STAR	1710		
6866	"Ill At Ease"	Vo- MB Trio 4 STAR	——			
8991	"Riff Raff"		4 STAR	1722		
8998	"Send Me the Pillow"		4 STAR	——		
7003	"I Can't Get Started"	Instrumental	4 STAR	1730		
7032	"Back Roads"	Vo- Jimmy Miller MB Trio	4 STAR	——		
7032	"Back Roads"		4 STAR	1736		
7036	"I Wanta Be Free"	Vo- Jimmy Miller	4 STAR	——		
7076	"You're No Longer Mine"	Vo- Frankie McWhorter	4 STAR	1750		
7077	"Crazy Dreams"	Vo- Jimmy McGraw	4 STAR	——		

MILLER BROS. BAND (EP Releases) Note: Some tracks are in main discography

A	"Ill At Ease"	Vo- MB Trio	MILLER BROS.	EP 20
	"Denver Hop"	Instrumental		——
B	"The Triflin' Kind"	Vo- Jimmy McGraw		——
	"The Keyboard Rag"	Instrumental		——
A	"Loco Choo Choo"	Vo- Jimmy McGraw		EP 29
	"Ramblin' Round"	Instrumental		——
B	"I Wanta Big Kiss"	Vo- Smiley Weaver		——
	"Travelin' "	Instrumental		——
	"Bummin' Around" + 3 unknowns			EP 32

MILLER BROS. BAND (Miscellaneous)

	"I Used to Walk in Chicago"	4 Star 45 rpm
	"Yes Yes Yes"	4 Star 45 rpm
	"Old Fashioned Christmas"	4 Star 45 rpm

APPENDIX TWO

No album or single 45 made by The Miller Brothers can be found at a music store today. They are the stuff of garage sales or collector sales, if the old plastic discs can be found at all.

The recordings were issued years ago, sold and never revived, except for a single long-play compact disc issued by a company in Europe, mentioned in the first chapter of this book.

When Leon Gibbs was busy making music, that is, writing, performing and recording it, he never paid much attention to ensuring that he had the registered copyright to what he was producing. As he looks back at a body of work, he admits that little of it is actually owned by him.

The first chapter of this book offers a glimpse at the way Leon thought about what he'd produced, an indication that for him it was never about money or fame, but about working, making a decent and honest living and having a good time of it. It also offers a glimpse at what's become of some the works he created. The European company that in 2002 was selling a CD featuring more than 20 songs performed by The Miller Brothers charged $15.95 plus shipping and handling to the United States. On the label of the CD, the company implied ownership of the music as written, performed and recorded. And it is possible that the European recording shop does own what it purports to own. But it also might not.

It almost certainly does not own them under United States copyright law. A search of the database maintained by the United States Copyright Office at its site on the World Wide Web produced the discovery that none of the works on the CD is copyrighted by a European firm. Likewise, a search of the Broadcast Music Inc. (BMI) database at its web site produced similar results – that is, the rights to the works are owned by a number of people. Only four of the songs were not in the United States Copyright Office database or the BMI database, and those are presumed to be owned by the author, Leon Gibbs. At any rate, Leon now has the copyright to those tunes.

The copyright situation is complicated not only by the fact that Leon was not very careful about registering his works when he wrote them, but also by the fact that many of the songs were apparently written by anonymous authors for use by artists signed to the Four Star music label. This is a complication because Four Star has long since gone out of business, and the evidence that remains appears to say that it signed over some rights to some music to other companies. For example, an Acuff-Rose music label owns the rights to some of The Miller Brothers tunes.

Searching was a bit complicated because Leon Gibbs went by the professional name of Leon Miller when he played with The Miller Brothers Orchestra and The Miller Brothers Band, and he also wrote some songs using the Miller surname. Searches have to be performed using both Gibbs and Miller as the author and performer names.

A final complication is that neither the U.S. Copyright Office nor BMI will certify anything found on their respective web sites. Instead, they suggest that absolute certainty concerning ownership of intellectual property can only come about when an author has a registration certificate in hand or after a costly search of the files by personnel in Washington and at BMI. At some point, that kind of search might be undertaken, but no such search had been made as of the publication date of this book.

Thus the reader will find no music or lyrics in this

volume. And it is unlikely that there will ever be an authorized reissue of The Miller Brothers music because of the copyright problems, because demand is limited and because Leon Gibbs has no interest in the project.

Those interested in hearing some authentic Leon Gibbs tunes with Leon on fiddle should direct their web browsers to www.m-bband.com on the Internet for a sample of his music.

APPENDIX THREE: BANDS

THE GIBBS BROTHERS
And
FIRST MILLER BROTHERS BAND

Leon Gibbs .... Violin
Sam Gibbs .... Guitar
Nat Gibbs .... Bass
Pete Martinez................. Steel Guitar
J.E. Gose .... Banjo and drums

THE MILLER BROTHERS
Post-World War II, Listing Every Player who Played in
The Group

Fiddle:

Leon Gibbs
Johnny Lytel
Troy Jordan
Dale Wilson
Jerry Byler
Frankie McWhorter
Bobby Rhoades

Bass:

Nat Gibbs
Paschalle Williams
Bill Taylor
Jim McGraw

Saxophone:

Forrest Fulcher
Bill Heath
Clyde Smith
Freddie Navarrete

Guitar:

Sam Gibbs
Tommy Bruce
Billy Thompson (3 times)
Bill Madry
Smiley Weaver (3 times)

Piano:

Pauline Fulcher
Madge Suttee Bolin
Curley Hollingsworth

Steel guitar:

Harvey Wilson
Dewayne Bass
Bill Jourdan

Trumpet:

Bob Womack
Lee Cochran

Drums:

Bobby Steed
Dutch Ingram

Vocalists:

Jay Starnes
(Several sang all the time)

THE MB TRIO

Leon Gibbs
Lee Cochran
Billy Thompson
Smiley Weaver

MILLER BROTHERS BUS DRIVERS

Bill Potts
Billy Peeler
Wayne Kindrick

(Curley Hollingsworth and Smiley Weaver were relief drivers)

LEON MILLER BAND
for
The Last Picture Show

Leon Gibbs .... Violin
Grady Solomon .... Guitar and vocalist
Jesse Moreno .... Drums
Bob Lemley .... Bass
Jimmy Boggs .... Lead guitar and vocalist

JIMMIE DAVIS BAND (The Sunshine Band)

Leon Gibbs .... Violin and emcee
Moon Mullins .... Piano and vocalist
C.B. Catruar .... Drums
Doc Guidry .... Violin and vocalist
Sonny Tramble .... Steel guitar
Johnny Patterson .... Guitar and vocalist

OVER THE HILL BAND

Wally Hendrixson .... Leader and steel guitar
Hank Whitson .... Bass
Mickey Stoddard .... Drums, trumpet
Jimmy Vie .... Guitar
Frank Farnsworth .... Fiddle

APPENDIX FOUR:
WHO PLAYED THE M-B CORRAL

BANDS THAT PLAYED THE M-B CORRAL
(An incomplete listing)

The Miller Brothers
Bob Wills & The Texas Playboys
The Texas Playboys
Johnny Lee Wills
Hank Thompson & The Brazos Valley Boys
Lou Walker Western Band
Hawkshaw Hawkins
Little Jimmy Dickens
Jimmie Davis
The Southernairs
Gordie Kilgore Orchestra
Toni Fenelli Orchestra
Ernie Fields Orchestra (an African-American group)
Fats Domino
Big Daddy Pat
Doc Jones
Shep Fields Orchestra
Tex Beneke Orchestra
Perez Prada Orchestra
B.B. King
Bo Diddley
Ike and Tina Turner
Joe Paul Nichols
Buck Owens
Billy Peeler and the Peeler Brothers
Johnny Patterson
Carl Smith
Hank Snow
Al Stidham

Boots Randolph
Maddox Brothers & Rose
Marty Robins
Johnny Rodriguez
Wade Ray
Curtis Patter
Charlie Pride
Webb Pierce
Rowe Brothers
Connie Kelley
Trini Lopez
Hank Locklin
Ferlin Huskey
Johnny Horton
Woodie Garman
David Holcomb
Johnny Duncan
Wichita Falls Symphony Orchestra
The Mad Medics
Chubby Checker
Bill Boyd
Lefty Frizzell
Conway Twitty
Elvis Presley
Tex Ritter
Gene Autry
Tommy Duncan
Goldie Hill
Little Richard
Willie Nelson
Bobby Blue Blan
Jerry Lee Lewis
Roger Miller
Ronnie Millsap

Merle Haggard
Ray Price
Etta James
James Brown
Freddie Fender
Ann Jones
Orville Couch
Don Cherry
Bozo Darnell
Max Ray Evans
Jack Frost
Andy Johnson
Billy Gray
Frank Goff
Mickey Gilley
Ray Irwin
Fulton Irby
Waylon Jennings
Ford Keeler
Elmer Lawrence
Leon McAuliff
Bill Mack
Rusty McDonald
Clint Cozart
Over the Hill Band
Jack Arnold and The Flames
Tommy Strange and The Features
Zeke Garcia
The Estrada Brothers
Shep Fields & His Rippling Rhythms
Rick & the Keens
Moe Bandy
Harry James
Boots Randolph

T. Texas Tyler
Dell Woods
Leon Rausch
Tommy Allsup
Wanda Jackson
Diana Ross
Leroy Van Dyke
Cubby Wise

REFERENCES

The Associated Press Writers and Photographers. *World War II*. New York: Henry Holt, 1989.

Brokaw, Tom. *The Greatest Generation*. New York: Dell, 1998.

Catalog. Sears-Roebuck and Co. Chicago, 1932.

Chance, Don. Interview with Leon Gibbs. April 2000.

_____. Interview with Sam Gibbs and Leon Gibbs. 1999.

_____. Personal communication to the author. December 4, 2002.

_____. Personal communication to the author. December 12, 2002.

Chase, Gilbert. *American Music: From the Pilgrims to the Present*. New York: McGraw-Hill, 1966.

Collier, James Lincoln. *The Making of Jazz: A Comprehensive History*. Boston: Houghton-Mifflin, 1978.

Copelin, Carroll. "Businessman Has Song in His Heart." *Wichita Falls Times* 23 October 1985: 1B.

Cost-of-Living Calculator. http://www.NewsEngin.com.

Cox, Jo Thornley. "Sam Gibbs: Wichita Falls' Own 'Music Man.'" *Wichita Falls Record News* 8 August 1980: 1B.

Dempsey, John Mark. *The Light Crust Doughboys Are On the Air*. Denton, Texas: North Texas UP, 2002.

Ewen, David. *All the Years of American Popular Music*. Englewood Cliffs, New Jersey: Prentice-Hall, 1977.

"Fifty Years of Progress." *Wichita Falls Times* 12 May 1957.

Gibbs, Nat. Personal communication to the author. February 2002.

Gordon, Lois G., and Alan Gordon. *American Chronicle: Six Decades in American Life*. New York: Atheneum, 1987.

Gregg, Louise. "The M-B Corral." *Wichita Falls Times* 15 July 1984: 1F.

Hasse, John Edward. *Jazz: The First Century*. New York: William Morrow, 2000.

Holcomb, David. Personal communication to the author. March 2002.

Information for National Advertisers. Wichita Falls, Texas: The Times Publishing Co., 1923.

King, Johnny. *An Insider's Guide to Understanding and Listening to Jazz*. New York: Walker, 1997.

Lay, Carole. Personal communication to the author. August 13, 2001.

McWhorter, Frankie. *Cowboy Fiddler in Bob Wills' Band.* Denton, Texas: North Texas UP, 1997.

Moore, Paula. Personal communication to the author. September 30, 2001.

Oermann, Robert K. *A Century of Country: An Illustrated History of Country Music.* New York: TV Books, 1999.

Schuller, Gunther. *The Swing Era: The Development of Jazz, 1930-1945.* New York: Oxford UP, 1989.

Stevens, Jack. Personal communication to the author. January 10, 2001.

Townsend, Charles R. *San Antonio Rose.* Urbana, Illinois: U of Illinois P, 1976.

Tricker, C.J. "Loco Choo Choo: The Miller Brothers." *The Roll Street Journal.* n.d.

Wheeler, Patsy. Personal communication to the author. August 10, 2001.

Zwonitzer, Mark, with Charles Hirshberg. *Will You Miss Me When I'm Gone? The Carter Family and Their Legacy in American Music.* New York: Simon & Schuster, 2002.